ABRAHAM LINCOLN, PUBLIC SPEAKER

Abraham

Lincoln PUBLIC SPEAKER

WALDO W. BRADEN

Louisiana State University Press
Baton Rouge and London

Designer: Sylvia Malik Loftin
Typeface: Electra
Typesetter: Focus Graphics

Library of Congress Cataloging-in-Publication Data
Braden, Waldo Warder, 1911–
    Abraham Lincoln, public speaker.

    Includes index.
    1. Lincoln, Abraham, 1809–1865—Oratory.   I. Title.
E457.2.B78   1988   973.7'092'4   88-6793
ISBN 0-8071-1433-2 (cloth)   ISBN 0-8071-1852-4 (paper)

Five chapters were previously published in different form in the *Lincoln Herald*: Chapter II, as "Abraham Lincoln's 'Little Engine,'" in LXXXIX (Summer, 1987), 66–70; Chapter III, as "'Kindly Let Me Be Silent,'" in LXXXVI (Winter, 1984), 195–202; Chapter VI, as "The Lasting Qualities of the Gettysburg Address," in LXXXVII (Summer, 1985), 35–38; Chapter VIII, as "Lincoln's Voice," in LXVII (Fall, 1965), 111–16; and Chapter IX, as "Lincoln's Delivery," in LXXXV (Fall, 1983), 167–74.

Frontispiece courtesy of the Library of Congress

The paper in this book meets the guidelines for permanence and durability of the Committee on Production Guidelines for Book Longevity of the Council on Library Resources. ∞

Louisiana Paperback Edition, 1993
02 01 00 99 98 97 96 95 94 93   5 4 3 2 1

CONTENTS

ACKNOWLEDGMENTS

My adventure through Lincolniana has extended over approximately twenty-five years, and I have sensed the spirit of Abraham Lincoln at the various shrines, historical displays, and specialized libraries devoted to him. In pursuing my research and developing insights, I have incurred many obligations to mentors, friends, and helpers who have guided me and provided encouragement and inspiration. To all who assisted me I wish to express my deep appreciation.

The Lincoln researcher has the advantages of a vast accumulation of materials and publications assembled by eyewitnesses and earwitnesses, archivists, biographers, collectors, critics, historians, dramatists, poets, psychologists, theologians, artists, and photographers. Most valuable are the compilations found in *Collected Works of Abraham Lincoln*, edited by Roy P. Basler and his staff, and *Lincoln Day By Day: A Chronology, 1809–1865*, edited by Earl Schenck Miers. The Warren L. Jones Lincoln Library, deposited in the Louisiana State University Library Special Collections (through the good offices of T. Harry Williams), has made readily available many fugitive Lincoln books and pamphlets.

I am much in the debt of the *Lincoln Herald*, published by Lincoln Memorial University, its editors, Joseph E. Suppiger and Edgar G. Archer, and its previous editor, Wayne Temple, now deputy director of the Illinois State Archives and a good friend. R. Gerald McMurtry and Mark E. Neely, Jr., and their staff at the Louis A. Warren Library, Fort Wayne, Indiana, have been helpful. I am grateful to the late Donald H. Ecroyd of Temple University for inviting me to participate in the Gettysburg Conference on Rhetorical Transactions in the Civil War Era, held on June 24 and 25, 1983, at Gettysburg College. Bernard Duffy of Clemson University and Halford Ryan of Washington and Lee University provided me with critical insights on some of my research.

Owen Peterson and Harold Mixon, colleagues at Louisiana State University, served as sounding boards and faithful listeners to my conversations about Lincoln. Likewise, Robert Gunderson of Indiana University and Herman Cohen of Pennsylvania State University have encouraged me.

I have had the advantages of assistance from Helen Braden Atkinson, who served as graphic artist, and the typists of PTS Word Processing, who cheerfully translated my difficult handwriting into beautiful typed copy. The staff of the Louisiana State University Press, including my copy editor, Michael Bounds, have skillfully guided me in the preparation of my manuscript and have improved my presentation.

INTRODUCTION
Literary Artist or Speaker?

Prior to 1858, if a reporter had made his way to almost any village in the central Illinois Eighth Judicial District (about 100 by 150 miles in area) and inquired about Abraham Lincoln, the reporter would have found many people eager to talk about this familiar character. They would have variously described him as a plain, perhaps even ugly, man of the people, a poor white Kentuckian, or an all-around westerner. They would have identified him as a storyteller, a lawyer, a talkative Whig, and an entertaining stump speaker—a good person to have on one's side in a lawsuit or to give sound advice about contracts, divorces, land titles, wills, or politics. They would have reported seeing the Springfield lawyer in the county seat or en route along country roads, attending court throughout the district—a pace that he maintained for twenty years.

But no one, even the editor of the local newspaper, would have called him an orator, a political philosopher, or a writer—not Honest Abe Lincoln. And even his best friends would have laughed at the suggestion that this politician might someday be president of the United States and commander of the armies of the nation.

Had the reporter asked Honest Abe for his opinion of what his friends and neighbors had said about him, he would have modestly agreed with their assessments, after telling a story or two, and confirmed that he had little desire to change or to give up his hard travels and seek an easier life. He might, however, have admitted he had a "taste" for serving, at some time, in the United States Senate.

This lawyer who has become a revered figure the world over deserves to be discussed from the standpoint of how he was viewed by his neighbors and himself before his rise to greatness, when he was above all a public speaker. Sometimes admirers and scholars, forgetting how Lincoln regarded himself, elevate him to the status of literary figure, assign to him a secondary role as a speaker, and ignore his

1

context, thus providing a one-sided view of his career. Historians and critics, concentrating on the First and Second Inaugural Addresses, the Gettysburg Address, selected state papers, and letters, have gone so far as to declare the assassinated president "a master of words" and "the most gifted writer among American statesmen of all times." The historian T. Harry Williams thought that among speakers of his time Lincoln was "a second-rate figure," but that as a writer, he "stands in the front rank of those few masters of language who have stirred men's emotions and moved them to action with the magic of words." Likewise, in a sweeping pronouncement, Herbert Joseph Edwards and John Erskine Hankins asserted that "Lincoln could never deliver an extemporaneous speech that was not less than mediocre." Not stopping there, they added: "Decidedly Lincoln was not an orator. He was something else—a literary artist—and he could work only with the tool of the literary artist, his pen." They imply that they missed in Lincoln the eloquence that they found in the speeches of Daniel Webster, Stephen A. Douglas, Charles Sumner, and Edward Everett.[1]

Such fascination with Lincoln as a stylist has come from "the misleading perspective of hindsight" and perhaps also from a slightly myth-encrusted perception. Granted, the claims about Lincoln's literary excellence have great merit; they have also served to obscure and to shift attention away from the historical Lincoln, the real man who was first a struggling citizen of Springfield, then a busy country lawyer, a shrewd and ambitious politician, a rugged campaigner for the young Republican party, and finally a successful wartime leader of the Union. This adoration of the writings of the sixteenth president as literature has served to minimize or obscure the fact that Lincoln first won attention on the platform, where he was principally concerned with persuading the common citizen. He was far too busy on the stump and in the courtroom to indulge in oratory for oratory's sake and had no desire to coin notable phrases to impress a reading public. He was a purposeful campaigner who argued that "this government cannot endure, permanently half-slave and half-free."[2]

1. Paul M. Angle, "Lincoln's Power with Words," *Abraham Lincoln Association Papers* (Springfield, Ill., 1935), 87; Richard N. Current, *The Lincoln Nobody Knows* (Westport, Conn., 1958), 8; T. Harry Williams (ed.), *Selected Writings and Speeches of Abraham Lincoln* (Chicago, 1943), xviii–liii; Herbert Joseph Edwards and John Erskine Hankins, "Lincoln the Writer: The Development of His Literary Style," *University of Maine Bulletin*, LXIV (April 10, 1962), 81.

2. David M. Potter, *Lincoln and His Party in the Secession Crisis* (New Haven, Conn., 1942), 315; Roy P. Basler (ed.), *The Collected Works of Abraham Lincoln* (9 vols.; New Brunswick, N.J., 1953), II, 461.

According to Lincoln's private secretaries, John G. Nicolay and John Hay, "Nothing would have more amazed him while he lived than to hear himself called a man of letters." In discussing "the effort and performance" of Lincoln, the British biographer Lord Charnwood saw in Lincoln's speeches against Douglas, not the "composition of a cloistered man of letters," but "the outpourings of an agitator upon the stump. . . . Lincoln's wisdom had to utter itself in a voice which would reach the outskirts of a large and sometimes excited crowd in the open air." Charnwood's generalization, which certainly applied to the Lincoln who spoke from 1854 to 1860, was confirmed by reporter Horace White of the Chicago *Press and Tribune*, who heard the Springfield lawyer many times and later wrote that it was "by restless competition and rough-and-tumble with Douglas and others that Mr. Lincoln acquired the rare power of eloquence." When he "was preparing himself unconsciously to be the nation's leader," said White, "the only means of gaining public attention was by public speech. The Press did not exist for him, or for the people among whom he lived. . . . If a man was to gain any popularity he must gain it by talking into the faces of the people. He must have a ready tongue and must be prepared to meet all comers and to accept all challenges." It was as a successful campaigner, concluded White, that Lincoln was "best understood by the common people and in turn best understood them." Those writers who assert that Lincoln's extemporaneous speeches never rose above the level of mediocrity give evidence that they have concentrated too much on the presidential rhetoric and too little on the hustings where the Illinois campaigner matched arguments with the best stump speakers and became the foremost spokesman of his party. His political pronouncements, first made in the towns and villages and byways, became the basic campaign documents of the young Republican party and helped bring it to power in 1860.[3]

3. John G. Nicolay and John Hay, *Abraham Lincoln: A History* (10 vols.; New York, 1904), X, 351; Lord Charnwood, *Abraham Lincoln* (New York, 1917), 133; Horace White, Introduction, in William H. Herndon and Jesse W. Weik, *Abraham Lincoln: The True Story of a Great Life* (2 vols.; New York, 1892), I, xix–xx.

I

"ANY POOR MAN'S SON"
The Public Image of Lincoln

The politician of today knows how important the right public image can be in winning elections. The boyish haircut of John F. Kennedy is said to have added to his appeal; Jimmy Carter made no secret of the fact that he was a born-again Christian; and Ronald and Nancy Reagan are adept at revealing signs of their conservatism. Some public figures pay thousands of dollars to promote attractive views of themselves, embracing a conviction that dates from Aristotle, who advised the Greeks that credibility (ethos) was the most powerful means of persuasion.

Although he lived before the advent of Madison Avenue, Abraham Lincoln learned the importance of his image as he worked his way upward from store clerk and hired hand to become an eminent figure throughout Illinois and among Republicans. During the period from 1830 to 1860 Lincoln actively projected the persona of a poor man's son, an underdog. "Keenly aware of his role as an exemplar of the self made man," Richard Hofstadter writes, Lincoln "played the part with an intense and poignant consistency that gives his performance the quality of high art. The first author of the Lincoln legend and the greatest of the Lincoln dramatists," concludes Hofstadter, "was Lincoln himself."[1]

In his first political handbill, addressed to the people of Sangamon County, Lincoln wrote on March 9, 1832: "I am young and unknown to many of you. I was born and have ever remained in the most humble walks of life. I have no wealthy or popular relations to recommend me. My case is thrown exclusively upon the independent voters in this county, and if elected they will have conferred a favor upon me. . . . But if the good people . . . shall see fit to keep me in the background, I have been too familiar with disappointments to be very much chagrined." Lincoln was not engaging in public confession

---

1. Richard Hofstadter, *American Political Tradition* (New York, 1948), 94.

or an expression of modesty, but pursuing votes, using the same theme of humility that he was to use throughout his life.[2]

It has frequently been said that he understood ordinary citizens because he was one of them and that, consequently, he was able to identify his causes with their aspirations and prejudices. While traveling about the state, politicking and practicing law, he became a familiar and favorite figure whose judgment was sought and greatly respected. Lawyers, judges, editors, and other opinion makers enjoyed his camaraderie, especially his storytelling. "The good people," fascinated by his quaintness, sensed his good humor and friendliness. He never changed his familiar habits and practices, continuing his rapport with his day-to-day associates even after he became associated with the aristocratic Whigs (one of whom, Mary Todd, he married) and began representing large corporations before the courts.

Lincoln was particularly mindful of the way he characterized himself in his confrontations with Stephen A. Douglas. In a speech in 1852 he recalled the "old times . . . when Judge Douglas was not so much greater than all the rest of us, as he now is." At another time Lincoln contrasted Douglas as "the giant" to himself as "a common mortal."[3] Sometimes when he was engaging in self-depreciation, Lincoln was also subtly ridiculing the 5-foot 4-inch senator for his bravado and display of affluence. In their 1858 debates, Lincoln never missed an opportunity to stress their differences. Sometimes it seemed that he was in many little ways reminding the common citizens that he was more like them than was the famous Douglas, who traveled in such high company in Washington. Douglas, cocky and urbane, did much to foster this impression.

In 1858, much in the limelight for his opposition to the Buchanan administration and as a presidential hopeful for 1860, Douglas made a dramatic return to Illinois to seek reelection. He opened in Chicago with a speech leveled mainly at Lincoln, his old rival, who had won attention with his remark that the Union could not exist half-slave and half-free. Douglas, in venting his determination to defeat his enemies, whether Buchanan Democrats (Danites) or Republicans, compared his intentions to those of the Russians at Sebastopol, who had fired "broad side" at their enemies, unconcerned about whether they

---

2. Roy P. Basler (ed.), *The Collected Works of Abraham Lincoln* (9 vols.; New Brunswick, N.J., 1953), I, 5–9.
3. *Ibid.*, II, 136.

hit Englishmen, Frenchmen, or Turks. "Just to think of it!" responded Lincoln. "I, a poor, kind, amiable, intelligent, gentleman, I am to be slain in this way. Why my friends, the Judge is not only, as it turns out, not a dead lion, nor even a living one—he is the rugged Russian bear."[4]

Newspapers throughout the country took great interest in covering the Illinois contest between the well-known Douglas and his rival, a newcomer to national politics. A special correspondent for the New York *Evening Post* wrote, in the August 27, 1858, edition, a revealing characterization of the candidates.

> Two men presenting wider contrasts could hardly be found as the representatives of the two great parties. Everybody knows Douglas, a short, thick-set, burly man, with large round head, heavy hair, dark complexion, and fierce bull-dog bark. Strong in his own real power, and skilled by a thousand conflicts in all the strategy of a hand-to-hand or a general fight. Of towering ambition, restless in his determined desire for notoriety; proud, defiant, arrogant, audacious, unscrupulous, "Little Dug," ascended the platform and looked out impudently and carelessly on the immense throng which surged and struggled before him. . . .
>
> The other—Lincoln—is a native of Kentucky, and of poor white parentage; and from his cradle has felt the blighting influence of the dark and cruel shadow which rendered labor dishonorable, and kept the poor in poverty, while it advanced the rich in their possessions. Reared in poverty and the humblest aspirations, he left his native state, crossed the line into Illinois, and began his career of honorable toil. At first a laborer, splitting rails for a living—deficient in education, and applying himself even to the rudiments of knowledge—he, too . . . began to achieve the greatness to which he has succeeded. . . . In physique he is the opposite to Douglas. Built on the Kentucky type, he is very tall, slender and angular, awkward even, in gait and attitude. His face is sharp, large-featured and unprepossessing. His eyes are deep set, under heavy brows; his forehead is high and retreating, and his hair is dark and heavy. In repose, I must confess that "Long Abe's" appearance is *not* comely.[5]

In one of his early speeches opposing Douglas, on July 17, 1858, in Springfield, Lincoln enjoyed making light of the differences between Douglas and himself.

> There is still another disadvantage under which we [Republicans] labor, and to which I will ask your attention. . . . Senator Douglas is of world wide renown. All the anxious politicians of his party . . . have been looking upon

4. *Ibid.*, II, 484–85.
5. Edwin Erle Sparks (ed.), *The Lincoln-Douglas Debates of 1858* (Springfield, Ill., 1908), 129–30.

him . . . to be the President of the United States. They have seen in his round, jolly, fruitful face, postoffices, landoffices, marshallships and cabinet appointments . . . bursting and sprouting out in wonderful exuberance ready to be laid hold of by their greedy hands. . . .

On the contrary nobody has ever expected me to be President. In my poor, lean, lank, face, nobody has ever seen that any cabbages were sprouting out. These are disadvantages all, taken together, that the Republicans labor under. We have to fight this battle upon principle, and upon principle alone. I am . . . made the standard-bearer in behalf of the Republicans. I was made so merely because there had to be someone . . . I being in no wise, preferable to any other one of the twenty-five—perhaps a hundred we have in the Republican ranks.[6]

What Lincoln said about himself was indeed an exaggeration, but it was consistent with his customary avowal of his "humble ability" and suggestion that others were more qualified than he.

In the first of his seven debates with Douglas, at Ottawa, Lincoln called himself "a small man" and Douglas "a man of vast influence so great that it is enough for many men to profess to believe anything when they once find out that Judge Douglas professes to believe it." Throughout the fall, Lincoln continued to stress the superiority of Douglas, letting the senator set the pace, determine the flow of argument, and play the aggressor. Following along, Lincoln continued his humble man approach.[7]

One of the most successful devices that advanced the humble man image and started Lincoln on the road to the White House was staged at the Republican state convention in Decatur, on May 9, 1860. In order to dramatize his beginnings and his frontier experience, Lincoln's promoters had his elderly cousin John Hanks march into the convention hall carrying two rails decorated with flags, streamers, and a placard reading:

> Abraham Lincoln
> The Rail Candidate
> For President in 1860
> Two rails from a lot by
> Thos. Hanks [sic] and Abe Lincoln . . .

Appearing surprised by this demonstration, Lincoln responded that whether the rails were taken from the fence he had built he could not

---

6. Basler (ed.), *Collected Works*, II, 506.
7. *Ibid.*, III, 27.

verify but that "he had mauled many and many better ones since he had grown to manhood."[8]

This episode gave impetus to Rail Splitter clubs and provided the Republican managers and cartoonists with a convenient theme by which to promote a presidential candidate who was not self-aggrandizing. Lincoln may actually have launched his Rail Splitter image a couple of months before when he spoke at New Haven, Connecticut. "I am not ashamed to confess that twenty-five years ago I was a hired laborer, mauling rails, at work on a flat boat—just what might happen to any poor man's son."[9]

Anyone encountering Lincoln must have felt that here was truly "a poor man's son." Ungainly, ugly, and countrified, he reinforced the public perception of him with his ill-fitting clothes, stovepipe hat, battered carpetbag, faded umbrella, and shawl. Even when he bought a new suit, as he did in 1860 for his appearance in New York at the Cooper Union for the Advancement of Science and Art, he still seemed wrinkled and disheveled. Dapper Douglas, spunky and fast moving, made his tall opponent seem even taller, slower, and quainter. Douglas gave the impression of being a planter or prosperous squire. His special train, with its booming cannon, added a dramatic and dynamic element to his campaign. His adversary, in contrast, was plain and persistent—Honest Abe. In a sense, Douglas could blame only himself when the Lincoln image gathered support.

"Abraham Lincoln's homely features," observed Gerald McMurtry, director of the Lincoln National Life Foundation, lent "themselves to pictorial exaggeration," and "his long angular figure" made him "the delight of cartoonists." As an important means of communication, these pictorial representations spread the Lincoln image widely throughout the reading public. In both North and South, and especially in England, the popular artists often worked into their drawings references to the Rail Splitter, with Lincoln carrying, riding, or waving a rail (twenty of the first thirty-six cartoons that author and editor Rufus Rockwell Wilson selected for his book illustrate this theme).[10]

A famous cartoon entitled "A 'Rail' Old Western Gentleman,"

---

8. *Ibid.*, IV, 48–49.
9. *Ibid.*, IV, 24; Wayne C. Temple, *Lincoln: The Railsplitter* (LaCrosse, Wis., 1961).
10. R. Gerald McMurtry, Introduction, in Rufus Rockwell Wilson, *Lincoln in Caricature* (New York, 1953), vi, 1–75.

drawn by Frank Bellew in July, 1860, pictured Lincoln's head mounted on a stick body of rails. Another, "The Rail Candidate," drawn by Louis Maurer and issued by Currier and Ives in August, 1860, pictured Lincoln astride a rail labeled "Republican platform." One end of the rail is carried by a black man, saying, "Dis Nigger strong and willin, but its awful hard work to carry Old Massa Abe on nothing but dis ere rail," and the other end is carried by Horace Greeley, declaring, "We can prove that you have split rails, and that will ensure your election to the Presidency." With a pained expression, Lincoln complains, "It is true I have split rails, but I begin to feel as if *this* rail would split me, its the hardest stick I ever straddled."[11]

The Cooper Union speech of February 27, 1860, showed a change in Lincoln's rhetorical stance. This appearance "was a critical venture, and he knew it," observed Lord Charnwood, an early biographer of Lincoln. "There was natural curiosity about this untutored man from the West. An exaggerated report of his wit prepared the way for probable disappointment. The surprise . . . awaited his hearers . . . prepared for a florid Western eloquence offensive to ears which were used to a less spontaneous turgidity; they heard instead a speech with no ornament." Said one source, "His style of speech and manner of delivery were severely simple." In fact, his thorough preparation for the Cooper Union appearance, including his decision to have a picture taken by Mathew Brady, indicated his growing concern about the necessity of improving the impression he made. From that occasion onward, Lincoln commenced to formalize his image; never again was he as spontaneous and relaxed as he had formerly been, engaging in the repartee of those who enjoyed participating in rallies. He became a reluctant speaker, making few speeches.[12]

En route to Washington in February, 1861, Lincoln responded to the adulation of official greeters and cheering crowds by discounting their attention. At these moments he expressed his appreciation for the nonpartisan support and tactfully implied that the cheering honored the office more than the man—a response that he used on at least seven occasions along the route.[13]

Likewise, he minimized his own importance and qualifications by referring to himself as "an humble instrument in the hands of the

11. *Ibid.*, Plate 7, pp. 14–15; Plate 15, pp. 30–31.
12. Lord Charnwood, *Abraham Lincoln* (New York, 1917), 155–56.
13. Basler (ed.), *Collected Works*, IV, 198, 205, 216, 225, 227.

Almighty" or by claiming, "With my own ability I cannot succeed without the sustenance of Divine Providence." He repeated this sentiment throughout his presidency. Upon leaving Springfield he had told his fellow townspeople, "Without the assistance of the Divine Being . . . I cannot succeed," and in the Second Inaugural Address, he said, "As God gives us to see the right, let us strive on to finish."[14]

Lincoln often stressed his inadequacy in coping with the enormity of the decisions before him. At Albany, New York, in February, 1861, he said that, considering himself "without mock modesty, the humblest of all individuals that have ever been elevated to the Presidency, I have a more difficult task to perform than any one of them." In the First Inaugural Address, he suggested that he had entered office "under great and peculiar difficulty—A disruption of the Federal Union." He also spoke of his dependence upon his "rightful masters, the American people," one of many references to the master-servant relationship.[15]

Sensitive to listener response, Lincoln must have become increasingly aware that the popular view of him as an amusing stump speaker did not carry the same persuasive power elsewhere that it had in the rural towns of Illinois. Earlier negative audience perceptions were brought home to him in a most painful way in the McCormick Reaper patent infringement case, tried in Cincinnati in 1855. When the case came to trial, two eastern lawyers brought in to bolster the defense were highly critical of the careless manner and disheveled appearance of the Illinois lawyer and froze him out of appearing before the court. Lincoln returned to Springfield humiliated, without ever having had an opportunity to deliver his carefully prepared argument.[16]

The pressures of increasing responsibilities, burdensome decisions, and impending disaster to the nation also motivated the sensitive Lincoln's reserve. He monitored his responses and assumed, as much as was possible, an impersonal role. He claimed little for himself, continuing in his attempts to project the same humility and modesty that had characterized him in Illinois. Few seemed to question his sincerity; they were more likely to declare him ignorant or crude. Critics either maligned his motives and virtues or asked whether it was

14. *Ibid.*, IV, 234, 236; VIII, 333.
15. *Ibid.*, IV, 190, 226.
16. William H. Herndon and Jesse W. Weik, *Herndon's Life of Lincoln* (New York, 1930), 285–86.

wise to entrust crucial decisions to someone of his poor background. Many southerners simply declared that Lincoln was not a gentleman and consequently was without honor.

Once in the White House, Lincoln retreated into silence and outwardly ignored much of the hate and censure leveled at him and his wife, as well as the excessive complaining of generals and government officials. His presidential duties and the executive routine screened him from some unpleasant exposure. Sometimes, when he felt the need to reply to a group or answer a challenge, he wrote a public letter, but of course he held no press conferences, a development of later presidents.[17]

Historian David Donald pronounced Lincoln "singularly ineffectual" in his public relations as president. "He never succeeded in selling himself—to the press, to the politicians, or to the people." Donald attributed Lincoln's success as president instead to his adroit manipulation of political and military forces.[18]

Like other presidents, Lincoln was soon made painfully cognizant of the delight taken by reporters and editors in playing up his idiosyncrasies and emphasizing his rustic background. They reported that Lincoln arrived in Washington in disguise, wearing either a Scottish costume or a dress. Even more vicious was the story that Lincoln had joked with his companion, Ward Lamon, and asked him to sing a ribald song while they viewed the Antietam battlefield site, where many soldiers had perished and near which many of the battle wounded were still housed. Of course, neither report was factual.[19]

Lincoln recognized his problems with reporters, and thus at Frederick, Maryland, on October 4, 1862, he excused himself for not speaking. "Every word is so closely noted that it will not do to make trivial ones." At Gettysburg, he explained his lack of response to a call for an impromptu reply. "In my position it is somewhat important that I should not say any foolish things."[20]

Some of the bitterest attacks on Lincoln, contributing to his public image, came from cartoonists, who passed off their venomous impressions as ironic or sardonic fun or as the customary fare of the press. In their illustrations of newsworthy events, depictions of the Rail Splitter

17. Basler (ed.), *Collected Works*, IV, 264.
18. David Donald, *Lincoln Reconsidered* (New York, 1961), 57–58.
19. Benjamin P. Thomas, *Abraham Lincoln: A Biography* (New York, 1952), 244–45; Mark E. Neely, Jr., *Abraham Lincoln Encyclopedia* (New York, 1982), 214.
20. Basler (ed.), *Collected Works*, V, 450; VII, 17.

soon gave way to portrayals of a skinny, bearded, long-legged figure, often dressed in a manner suggesting Uncle Sam, with striped pants and starred coat or vest, or perhaps a military figure or a pirate wearing a three-cornered hat. Lincoln's rough boots were a favorite target of the cartoonists.[21]

The British cartoons that appeared in *Punch* or *Fun* were always spicier than their American counterparts and, of course, anti-Union. They represented Lincoln "as a bearded ruffian, a repulsive compound of malice, vulgarity, and cunning" and often pictured him being lectured by a sturdy John Bull. One of the cruelest cartoons, dated December 3, 1864, after Lincoln had won a second term, showed Columbia gripping the arm of the president, saying: "Lincoln, you have brought me to this, yet I have not flinched to perform my part of the contract. I still cling to you that you may fulfill yours. You have swollen the earth with the blood of my children. Show me what I am to gain by this, or look for my dire vengeance in the future."[22]

What effect such cartoons had upon Lincoln is difficult to say. They did represent the attitudes of many editors and newspaper owners as well as peace Democrats, Confederate sympathizers, and Unionists who thought that Lincoln was doing a poor job. Lincoln ignored much of their sting but sometimes laughed at a clever drawing and its sardonic humor.

To the end of his life Lincoln never lost the honest or humble image that he had launched years before in Sangamon County. In 1865, in both affection and derision, he remained Old Abe, the Rail Splitter. The New York *Herald*, highly critical of him for much of his presidency, showed a change in its point of view with his second inauguration. Its editorial fittingly summarized the Lincoln image. "The republican wire pullers . . . were looking for a convenient instrument, when they picked up their master in that good-natured, uncouth, ungainly, and unpretending Illinois rail splitter, Abraham Lincoln. . . . He is a most remarkable man. He may seem to be the most credulous, docile, and pliable of back woods men, and yet when he 'puts his foot down he puts it down firmly,' and cannot be budged. He has proved himself, in his quiet way, the keenest of politicians."[23]

21. Wilson, *Lincoln in Caricature*, 167–77 *passim*.
22. William S. Walsh (ed.), *Abraham Lincoln and London Punch* (New York, 1909), 23–89 *passim*.
23. Mitgang, *Press Portrait*, 436–38.

My discussion has been limited mainly to Lincoln's own rhetorical efforts to foster and use his humble man image. A more inclusive review might also have discussed the propaganda devices of advisers, friends, managers, reporters, promoters, and hucksters who sought to sell Lincoln through assorted badges, buttons, banners, cartoons and line drawings, sheet music, staged parades and social meetings, costumes, printed and painted portraits, statuary, and other mementoes, such as rails. Further, Harold Holzer, Gabor S. Boritt, and Mark E. Neely, Jr., suggest in their enlightening book *The Lincoln Image* that by 1863 "*Carte-de-visite* photographs, woodcuts in the nationally distributed New York illustrated newspapers, and portraits purchased at print shops, bookstores, and newspaper offices, through the mail, or from itinerant agents had turned the unknown face of a western politician into the best-known face in the United States in a brief period of time."[24] All of these promotional stratagems complicate the attempt to determine the evolution of a public figure's image.

Aristotle made an important point about evaluating a speaker's art, particularly as it applied to image. He suggested that the rhetorical critic must distinguish between artistic (conscious) and inartistic (unconscious) means of persuasion, giving plaudits only to the speaker who consciously incorporates a given means in his rhetoric. One contemporary example clarifies the Aristotelian concern. Dwight D. Eisenhower was tremendously popular with American voters when he was elected president in 1952, but he was a mediocre speaker whose effectiveness lay not in his fluency or eloquence but in his reputation as a five-star general who had led the Allies to victory.

The influence of Lincoln's humble man image, created and furthered by many sources, makes pertinent a query about his own means of persuasion. Was Lincoln, who was truly plain and a "poor man's son," naturally persuasive because listeners responded unconsciously and identified with him? Or did Lincoln "play a part" and emphasize his humbleness? From what is known about his driving ambition, his "little engine," it seems very likely that Lincoln had much to do with building his appeal around his personality and background. This conclusion is particularly true of the formative stage of his public life in Illinois. Although he never lost his lifelong modesty and tact, Lincoln found it wise to alter his public image as

24. Harold Holzer, Gabor S. Boritt, and Mark E. Neely, Jr., *The Lincoln Image: Abraham Lincoln and The Popular Print* (New York, 1984), xvi.

president; he never during those years overtly played upon his simple beginnings.

In his two inaugural addresses and at Gettysburg, he modified his image (often inserted into his presentation most subtly) to fit the seriousness of each occasion. Much to the surprise of those who contended that he could not make a serious speech, Lincoln demonstrated that he was a polished rhetor who could produce ceremonial speeches that rank among the finest in the English language.

II

ABRAHAM LINCOLN'S "LITTLE ENGINE"
His Political Speaking, 1854–1860

"That man who thinks Lincoln calmly sat down and gathered his robes about him, waiting for the people to call him, has a very erroneous knowledge of Lincoln," reported William Herndon, his law partner and biographer. "He was always calculating, and always planning ahead. His ambition was a little engine that knew no rest."[1]

What we know about Abraham Lincoln as a campaigner is too often limited to what has been written about his seven famous debates with Stephen A. Douglas in 1858. "The confrontations on the Illinois prairies," wrote Robert W. Johannsen, "have often been wrenched out of time and place and invested with certain mythic qualities that converted a significant political contest into a timeless and epic struggle between good and evil." As a result, a distorted or incomplete picture emerges of how Lincoln performed at the hustings.[2]

The period from 1854 to 1860 encompassed four elections, over 175 speeches, and Lincoln's most intense and energetic politicking.[3] It was during nineteen months in the years 1854, 1856, 1858, 1859, and 1860 that Lincoln's strategies on the stump were particularly in evidence and that his national reputation as a masterful public speaker and debater grew. In contrast to his presidential years, when he was reluctant to speak publicly, these were years when he sought out audiences, usually spoke for two or three hours or more, and was most willing to accommodate almost any request to speak, even last-minute invitations. Much of the time, he was opposing the widely acclaimed Illinois senator Stephen A. Douglas and other formidable speakers.

1. William H. Herndon and Jesse W. Weik, *Herndon's Life of Lincoln* (New York, 1930), 304.
2. Robert W. Johannsen, "The Lincoln-Douglas Campaign of 1858," *Journal of the Illinois State Historical Society*, LXXII (Winter, 1980), 246.
3. This number has been determined by consulting Roy P. Basler (ed.), *The Collected Works of Abraham Lincoln* (9 vols.; New Brunswick, N.J., 1953), and Earl Schenck Miers (ed.), *Lincoln Day by Day: A Chronology, 1809–1865* (3 vols.; Washington, D.C., 1960), II.

An overview of these busy Lincoln years will help to get behind the "mythic qualities" of the Lincoln-Douglas debates in order to put them into perspective and to present an image nearer that of the real Lincoln.

1854

When he completed his one term (1847–1849) in the United States House of Representatives, a somewhat disillusioned Lincoln resumed his law practice in Springfield, Illinois, with, he said, a "greater earnestness than ever before." But his "little engine" moved him to change course in the congressional campaign of 1854. He explained that the repeal of the Missouri Compromise had aroused him to tackle national issues. In the Kansas-Nebraska problem, the repeal of the Missouri Compromise, and the ensuing sectional storm, Lincoln possibly saw cracks in the armor of his old rival Douglas. Considering that possibility, one historian has said that "Lincoln, stirred to the depths, was a different man from the easy going lawyer whose jokes were a byword in central Illinois."[4]

In 1854 Lincoln suggested that he had taken the stump "with no broader practical aim" than "to secure, if possible, the reelection of Hon. Richard Yates to Congress."[5] But herein Lincoln did not tell all, for he was very much interested in winning a United States Senate seat himself. True to his announced objective, Lincoln made five speeches in Yates's behalf, but it was when Douglas reappeared in the state that a changed Lincoln emerged.

Now picking up steam, Lincoln launched a campaign that carried him through the next four elections, with Douglas as the primary target. Lincoln was in Bloomington on September 25 to hear the senior Illinois senator and to reply on the following day. The controversy continued in Springfield, with Douglas again speaking and Lincoln replying the day after in what Paul Angle has called Lincoln's "first great speech." The reporter Horace White, of the Chicago *Press and Tribune*, gives us a picture of the Rail Splitter that day.

Mr. Lincoln was in his shirt sleeves when he stepped on the platform. I observed that, although awkward, he was not in the least embarrassed. He

4. Basler (ed.), *Collected Works*, IV, 67; Paul M. Angle, "Lincoln's Power with Words," *Abraham Lincoln Association Papers* (Springfield, Ill., 1935), 72.
5. Basler (ed.), *Collected Works*, IV, 67.

began in a slow and hesitating manner, but without any mistakes of language, dates, or facts. It was evident that he had mastered his subject, that he knew what he was going to say, and that he knew he was right. He had a thin, high-pitched falsetto voice of much carrying power, that could be heard a long distance in spite of the bustle and tumult of a crowd. He had the accent and pronunciation peculiar to his native state, Kentucky. Gradually he warmed up with his subject, his angularity disappeared, and he passed into that attitude of unconscious majesty.[6]

Twelve days later, at Peoria on October 16, the third confrontation took place, with Lincoln once more answering Douglas. Listeners agreed that the Peoria speech was largely a repetition of what Lincoln had extemporized earlier in Springfield. They encouraged him to reproduce the speech for publication, and it became Lincoln's first selected campaign document. It contained the constructive case, that is, the basic arguments, that he would draw upon for six years and bring to fruition at his Cooper Union appearance in 1860. He opposed the repeal of the Missouri Compromise because it permitted the spread of what he considered the immoral institution of slavery. According to a rumor circulated at the time, Lincoln and Douglas agreed after Peoria to curtail their speaking during the remaining weeks of the canvass, but it is more likely that their clashes ceased because Douglas developed severe hoarseness. Both made further speeches, with Lincoln appearing at Urbana (October 24), Chicago (October 27), and Quincy (November 1).[7]

The 1854 struggle, brief as it was, set the pattern for subsequent encounters, with Douglas as the protagonist, taking the lead, setting the schedules, proving an exciting adversary, and opening up an ever-expanding audience to Lincoln. Asserting himself as the leading anti-Nebraska Whig (but not, at first, as a Republican), Lincoln dogged his opponent, unceasingly denouncing the spread of slavery in the territories. After the election he admitted that he had got into his head "to try to be United States Senator." In the 1855 vote for United States senatorship in the Illinois legislature, Lincoln led on the first ballot with forty-four votes, three more than his nearest rival but not enough to be elected. Finally, after nine subsequent tries with dwindling

6. Horace White, "Abraham Lincoln in 1854," *Transactions of the Illinois State Historical Society, 1908*, No. 13 (1909), 32.

7. Angle, "Power with Words," 73; Ernest E. East, "The 'Peoria Truce': Did Douglas Ask for Quarter?" *Journal of the Illinois State Historical Society*, XXIX (April, 1936), 70–75.

votes, Lincoln threw his support to anti-Nebraska Democrat Lyman Trumbull, who was elected.[8]

1856

The presidential campaign of 1856, a pivotal one for Lincoln, showed his "little engine" picking up speed. The first pivotal factor of the campaign was his affiliation with the new Republican party, which he had earlier shied away from because he feared being associated with politicians who had expressed strong abolitionist biases. On May 29 he became a Republican when he attended, as a delegate, the "fusion" Anti-Nebraska Convention at Bloomington (the convention call had avoided the word *republican*). At this meeting, which according to one authority "sounded the death knell of Illinois Whiggery," Lincoln delivered what William Herndon called "the grand effort" of Lincoln's life—an oration that helped to make him "the leader of the new party" and that constituted the second pivotal factor in his campaign. According to contemporary accounts, an impassioned Lincoln was so persuasive and eloquent that admirers and reporters "listened as though transfixed" and consequently did not record what he said. The mystery is that Lincoln himself did not later transcribe this powerful pronouncement (now known as the "Lost Speech"), as he did in other cases. Perhaps Republican strategists were willing to let it fade away because they feared that it would create discord at a moment when they were attempting to draw together diverse elements of anti-Democratic sentiment.[9]

The third pivotal factor in this campaign was that Lincoln kept alive the possibility of his seeking Douglas' Senate seat. When, at the Anti-Nebraska Editors' Convention in Decatur on February 22, his friend Richard Oglesby toasted Lincoln as "our next candidate for the United States Senate," Lincoln responded that he liked the idea. During the fall, he established himself among important Republicans throughout Illinois and helped to strengthen the party's organization. In the five-month campaign (from June 4 to November 4), Lincoln delivered

---

8. Basler (ed.), *Collected Works*, II, 286, 288, 289, 290, 304.
9. Reinhard H. Luthin, "Abraham Lincoln Becomes a Republican," *Political Science Quarterly*, CIX (September, 1944), 437; Harry Pratt, "Abraham Lincoln in Bloomington," *Journal of the Illinois State Historical Society*, XXIX (April, 1936), 55; Elwell Crissey, *Lincoln's Lost Speech: The Pivot of His Career* (New York, 1967). In 1896 Henry C. Whitney attempted a reconstruction that the editors of *Collected Works*, II, 341, declared unworthy of serious consideration.

more than fifty speeches in twenty-eight scattered counties.[10] During this time, he continued his law practice but scheduled political appearances whenever convenient. He frequently addressed rallies in towns where court was convened, speaking four times in Bloomington (May 28, 29, September 12 and 16), four times in Urbana (June 23, September 17, October 20, 21) and six times in his hometown of Springfield (June 10, August 2, September 6, 25, October 29, and 31). The other seventy percent of his stumping stretched from Galena, in the far northwest, to Belleville, just south of Saint Louis, and to Lawrenceville and Olney, in the southeast. Adopting a strategy that he would continue in 1858, Lincoln concentrated his greatest efforts in the five central congressional districts, where the Republicans had to battle Know-Nothings as well as Democrats. (He could not have kept up his active schedule without the railroad lines, which had become a new force in Illinois politics since 1850.)

As a presidential elector, Lincoln did his best to elect both John C. Frémont and the state ticket, but he was successful only in the latter. In addition to gaining statewide recognition as a Republican leader and a hard campaigner, Lincoln began attracting interest outside the state. At the Republican National Convention on June 17, the Illinois delegation nominated him for the vice-presidency, and though he received 110 votes on the first ballot, he lost to the eventual choice, William L. Dayton of New Jersey. He was also invited to address a great Republican rally at Kalamazoo, Michigan, on August 27, his first out-of-state campaign appearance as a Republican.[11]

All of Lincoln's 1856 speeches were extemporaneous. He later wrote that not one of them "so far as he remember[ed]" was put into print. Neither Lincoln nor the newspapers must have considered any of them worth preserving for future citation.[12]

1858

The 1858 senatorial campaign involved Lincoln's most important political speaking, without which he probably would never have become president. The two previous canvasses had served as mere

10. Basler (ed.), *Collected Works*, II, 333. In a biographical statement prepared for John L. Scripps, Lincoln recorded, "In the canvass of 1856, Mr. L. made over fifty speeches." *Ibid.*, IV, 67. I can account for only forty-six.

11. Thomas I. Starr, *Lincoln's Kalamazoo Address* (Detroit, 1941).

12. At the time, Lincoln was unaware that the Kalamazoo speech had been published in full in a Michigan newspaper.

dress rehearsals for this main performance. Lincoln, now a mature, seasoned politician, was ready to do battle on equal terms with the cocky, popular Stephen A. Douglas, who, despite having been scarred by his recent opposition to President James Buchanan's program for Kansas, was being touted as a prime prospect for the 1860 Democratic presidential nomination. To defeat Douglas at home was an excellent way to gain national recognition for both Lincoln and the infant Republican party.

The Illinois Republicans had sufficient strength to challenge Douglas, who had become prominent in the Senate. They had a strong statewide organization that drew together Free-Soil Democrats, Whigs, German-Americans, and abolitionists; and they had tested themselves, and passed the test, by electing almost a complete slate of state officers in 1856. They had demonstrated strong followings in the two northern congressional districts (fifteen counties) and had a good chance of winning in the five central districts. They conceded to the Democrats only the two southern districts, known as Little Egypt (twenty-six counties). Also, the Republicans had a shrewd, ambitious challenger in Lincoln, who, through his itinerating, had won face-to-face recognition among the rank and file and who understood well his rival Douglas.

Lincoln clearly advanced a strong position in his House Divided speech, thoughtfully prepared and read at the state convention in Springfield on June 16. Obviously, he intended this speech to be the basis for future statements, because he had it published in the exact form in which he delivered it. In this address Lincoln stated a position—that the spread of slavery must be arrested—from which he never retreated and which became the focus of much of Douglas' attack on him.[13]

The two candidates introduced innovations in the 1858 canvass that distinguished it from the two previous contests and changed future campaigns as well. The nomination of Lincoln was unique in that he received ninety-five county convention endorsements, he was nominated by a state convention, and he delivered a formal acceptance speech. Anticipating the popular election of senators, still many years in the future, Lincoln and Douglas appealed directly to the voters,

13. Herndon and Weik, *Life of Lincoln*, 326–27; Horace White, *The Lincoln and Douglas Debates: An Address Before the Chicago Historical Society, February 17, 1914* (Chicago, 1914), 16.

Congressional map of Illinois, 1858, showing the locations of the Lincoln-Douglas
debates.

Originally published in Edwin Erle Sparks, *The Lincoln-Douglas Debates of 1858* (Springfield, 1908), 71.
Permission to publish granted by the Illinois State Historical Library.

acting as if the election were in the hands of the voters and not the state legislature.[14]

Putting his law practice on hold, Lincoln spared no effort to win, devoting all of his time and resources to stumping. On the basis of a detailed, county-by-county analysis of the 1856 voting, it is evident that he concentrated much more than previously on key counties in central Illinois. By November, he had spoken in thirty-nine of Illinois' one hundred counties (Douglas had appeared in fifty-seven). In the majority (twenty-four) Lincoln spoke only once, but in critical counties he appeared more often: three times each in Sangamon and Madison and four times in Hancock.[15]

As in his 1854 campaign, Lincoln preferred to follow Douglas about the state, saying that his "recent experience" showed that speaking at the same place where Douglas had spoken the day before provided him the opportunity to give "a concluding speech on him."[16] When Douglas appeared at the Tremont House in Chicago on July 9, Lincoln was there to listen and to reply the following night. Lincoln listened intently to Douglas on July 16 in Bloomington and on July 17 in Atlanta, and gave a second reply on the evening of Douglas' fourth address, on July 17 in Springfield. He continued giving "concluding" speeches, both in Clinton on July 27 and in Monticello on July 29, and supporters assumed that he would continue this tagging along throughout the fall. In fact, the Republican state committee issued a schedule that put Lincoln wherever Douglas had spoken the day before. The joint canvass was formalized when on July 28 Douglas agreed to share the same platform with Lincoln in the seven remaining congressional districts. In addition to the seven 3-hour debates, Lincoln continued to follow Douglas, speaking in each of the twenty-nine places where the Little Giant had appeared.

Once Lincoln had formally opened his campaign, on August 12 at Beardstown, he stayed on the trail, returning to Springfield only four times, usually for less than a day, on Sundays. Lincoln seldom lingered anywhere for more than a day. Sometimes he stayed with a

14. Harry E. Pratt, *The Great Debate* (Springfield, 1955), 4.

15. *Illinois State Register*, November 23, 1858, quoted in Edwin Erle Sparks (ed.), *The Lincoln-Douglas Debates of 1858* (Springfield, Ill., 1908), 529, vol. III of *Collections of the Illinois State Historical Library*; Abraham Lincoln to Norman Judd, October 24, 1858, in Basler (ed.), *Collected Works*, III, 332.

16. Abraham Lincoln to William Fithian, September 3, 1858, in Basler (ed.), *Collected Works*, III, 84–85.

supporter overnight, but more often he checked in at a primitive village hotel. It is not known how often his hotel bills were paid by the local committees, but at Macomb on October 26, his room bill of $2.50 at the Randolph House was charged to the Lincoln Club.[17]

On the whole, Lincoln was his own campaign manager, keeping up a stream of letters to those responsible for local arrangements. Whenever necessary, he modified his travel plans. Eager to offend no one and to reach as many voters as possible, Lincoln generously complied with the wishes of local supporters, adding appearances, seeking few comforts, and adjusting to the rigors of outdoor speaking in all kinds of weather. Since he had served as a railroad attorney, he may have sometimes used passes when traveling by train, but seldom did he find schedules that fit his ever-changing needs. His accommodations, moreover, were not as commodious as those of Douglas, who, with his wife, rode in a "gorgeously decorated" private coach, pulling a flatcar on which was mounted a twelve-pounder to boom forth when he arrived. Lincoln usually came along after Douglas on slower carriers and even on freight trains that were sometimes sidetracked to let Douglas flash by. To reach a given point, Lincoln might have to utilize two or three different kinds of transportation and endure wearisome delays while changing rail lines. During the campaign, he covered 4,350 miles (350 by boat, 600 by carriage, and 3,400 by train) and delivered 63 speeches, including those in the debates. He spent about $1,000, compared to Douglas' more lavish output, estimated to be as much as $50,000.[18]

The flavor of the stumping is reflected in Lincoln's activities in the nine days preceding the Ottawa debate. Leaving Springfield on the evening of August 11, on the Great Western Railroad he traveled west to the Illinois River port of Naples. There he boarded the side-wheel packet *Sam Gaty*, which carried him upriver overnight. At Beardstown (which Douglas had visited the previous day) he gave his first two-hour speech. The next day, still tagging along after Douglas, he boarded the steamer *Editor* and headed upriver again for Havana. Horace White gave an account of the trip.

Several of his old Whig friends were on board, and the journey was filled with politics and story telling. . . . In the latter Branch of human affairs, Mr.

17. Miers (ed.), *Lincoln Day by Day*, II, 234.
18. Henry Clay Whitney, *Life on the Circuit with Lincoln* (Caldwell, Idaho, 1940), 410; Pratt, *Great Debate*, 5–9.

Lincoln was most highly gifted. From the beginning to the end of our travels the fund of anecdotes never failed, and wherever we happened to be all the people within ear-shot would begin to work their way up to this inimitable storyteller. His stories were always *apropos* of something going on. . . . Although the intervals between the meetings were filled up brimful with mirth in this way, Mr. Lincoln indulged very sparingly in humor in his speeches.[19]

At 2 P.M. on August 14, Lincoln made a second two-hour speech. On August 16 he retraced his route downriver to Bath to answer a last-minute request for a speech, his third. On August 17, back on the river, he returned to Havana and continued by carriage to Lewistown for another two-hour appearance. Following that rally, he pressed on to Canton by rig. The next day he went to Peoria to deliver a final two-hour speech in the town square and to attend the Fourth District Republican Congressional Convention. On August 20, Lincoln took the Peoria-Bureau Valley Railroad to Morris to spend the night as the guest of Judge William T. Hopkins. The morning of the debate, Lincoln boarded the Chicago and Rock Island Railroad for Ottawa. Traveling "so unostentatiously," reported Henry Whitney, he gave the appearance of "the humblest commercial traveler. He sat with me throughout the journey; and . . . exhibited not the slightest trace of excitement or nervousness. . . . We talked about matters other than the impending debate."[20]

From August 12 through 21, Lincoln had faced crowds almost every day and could have had little time to prepare for the first debate; consequently, he had to draw upon what he had assembled while in Springfield between July 28 and August 11.[21] The seven debates were only a small part of Lincoln's political speaking. He and Douglas were striving to reach as many voters as possible in critical areas. Between Ottawa and the second debate, at Freeport (August 27), in five days Lincoln made five speeches; he made thirteen more prior to Jonesboro (September 15) and Charleston (September 18), another ten leading up to Galesburg (October 7), and four more en route to Quincy (October 13). After the seventh debate, at Alton (October 15), Lincoln spoke twelve more times before the election on November 2.

19. Horace White, Introduction, in William H. Herndon and Jesse W. Weik, *Abraham Lincoln: The True Story of a Great Life* (2 vols.; New York, 1892), II, 101.

20. Whitney, *Life on the Circuit*, 408.

21. The details of the nine days are drawn from Miers (ed.), *Lincoln Day by Day*, II, 224–25; Sparks (ed.), *Lincoln-Douglas Debates*, 128–45 *passim*; and Pratt, *Great Debate*, 12–14.

For the Douglas Democrats and the Republicans, the 1858 confrontations became a contest of showmanship and spectacle, designed to demonstrate enthusiasm for the candidates. In their efforts to outdo each other, the two political factions vented their exuberance through shouting, singing, mottoes, badges, banners, flags, floats, booming cannons, marching bands, long processions, torchlight parades, and troupes of young ladies dressed in patriotic costumes. In the spirit of the occasion, the two candidates usually timed their arrivals to increase the dramatic effect and heighten excitement. Along the way, they had picked up shouting partisans, who went along to enjoy the fun and be near their favorite candidate.[22]

Providing a view of this atmosphere, Carl Schurz recounts a scene on the train en route to Quincy.

All at once, after the train had left a way-station, I observed a great commotion among my fellow-passengers, many of whom jumped from their seats and pressed eagerly around a tall man who had just entered the car. They addressed him in the most familiar style: "Hello, Abe! How are you?" and so on. And he responded in the same manner: "Good-evening, Ben! How are you, Joe? Glad to see you, Dick!" and there was much laughter at some things he said, which, in the confusion of voices, I could not understand. "Why," exclaimed my companion, the committee-man, "there's Lincoln, himself!" He pressed through the crowd and introduced me to Abraham Lincoln, whom I then saw for the first time. . . .

He received me with an off-hand cordiality, like an old acquaintance . . . and we sat down together. In a somewhat high-pitched but pleasant voice . . . [he] talked in so simple and familiar a strain, and his manner and homely phrase were so absolutely free from any semblance of self-consciousness or pretension of superiority, that I soon felt as if I had known him all my life, and we had very long been close friends. He interspersed our conversations with all sorts of quaint stories, each of which had a witty point applicable to the subject in hand, and not seldom concluded an argument in such a manner that nothing more was to be said.[23]

When a candidate arrived in town, a local delegation welcomed him with fanfare and enthusiasm, and a procession marched with the orator and his party to a local hotel where other supporters waited to greet him. After he had eaten lunch and rested, they escorted him on to the place of the debate.

Great crowds impatiently milled about and overran the little towns

22. Newspaper accounts quoted in Sparks (ed.), *Lincoln-Douglas Debates*.
23. Carl Schurz, "Reminiscences of a Long Life," *McClure's Magazine*, XXVIII (January, 1907), 253.

that hosted the debates—Ottawa, Freeport, Jonesboro, Charleston, Galesburg, Quincy, and Alton. People came on foot and horseback, in wagons and carriages, by riverboats and excursion trains. Some were members of delegations from nearby cities and even the adjoining states of Indiana, Iowa, and Missouri. Partisan reporters exaggerated the events, as well as their estimates of the size of the crowds, suggesting as many as 12,000 to 20,000 people. More likely, five of the debates drew as many as 10,000 to 15,000, but at Alton there were about 4,000, and at remote Jonesboro, 1,200 to 1,500.[24]

When the first speaker was introduced, the listeners pressed in around the speaker's stand, sitting or standing in the hot sun (Ottawa) or in the chilly wind and rain (Freeport, Galesburg, and Quincy). For three hours they listened, sometimes cheering and shouting, sometimes boisterous and rowdy—at times even fighting. The speaker was taxed to take command, to make himself heard at the far reaches of the crowd, and to cope with unexpected questions, side comments, jeers, laughter, and applause. Lincoln and Douglas attempted to stay within their time limits and asked the listeners not to waste their time. They were well aware that their remarks were being transcribed by "phonographic reporters" and that what they said would be quoted in newspapers throughout Illinois and beyond. The debates marked the first occurrence of such an extensive use of shorthand in covering a political canvass.[25]

Seasoned by strenuous years on the Eighth Judicial Circuit, Lincoln cheerfully made the best of the tedium of constant travel. Whenever possible, he heard Douglas, read the newspapers, wrote letters to influential Republicans, reviewed his notes for his next speech, and picked up snatches of sleep. Usually he paused for a day's rest on Sundays.

Carl Schurz described Lincoln's appearance on tour.

On his head he wore a somewhat battered "stove-pipe hat." His neck emerged, long and sinewy from a white collar turned down over a thin black necktie. His lank, ungainly body was clad in a rusty black frock-coat with sleeves that should have been longer; but his arms appeared so long that the sleeves of a "store" coat could hardly have been expected to cover them all the way down to the wrists. His black trousers, too, permitted a very full view of

24. Sparks (ed.), *Lincoln-Douglas Debates.* The conservative estimates are supported by Mark E. Neeley, Jr., *Abraham Lincoln Encyclopedia* (New York, 1982), 4, 51, 117, 123, 167, 228, 249.

25. Sparks (ed.), *Lincoln-Douglas Debates,* 75–84.

his large feet. On his left arm he carried a gray woolen shawl, which evidently served him for an overcoat in chilly weather. His left hand held a cotton umbrella of the bulging kind, and also a black satchel that bore the marks of long and hard usage. His right he had kept free for hand-shaking.[26]

Brief glimpses of Lincoln during the fall suggest that he had pleasant moments: listening to Douglas in Chicago and Bloomington; observing the scenery along the Illinois River from a steamer and visiting with the boat captain; meeting and reminiscing with fellow Black Hawk War veterans at Bath; attending political conventions at Peoria, Tremont, and Augusta; riding to the debate site at Freeport in a Conestoga wagon; staying with old friends such as David Davis of Bloomington; perusing the *Congressional Globe* in the office of Judge John Moses in Winchester; swapping stories with Horace White, who traveled with him for much of the tour; seeing relatives in Coles County; visiting with James W. Grimes, a former Whig governor of Iowa, in Burlington, Iowa; and being cajoled by friends and reception committees.[27]

When the election was over, Lincoln seemed as vigorous as ever, lean, tanned, and hearty, in contrast to the haggard winner, Douglas, who had drunk too much bad whiskey, overspent to the extent that he imperiled his resources, pursued a more exhausting schedule, and developed hoarseness and a throat infection. Lincoln must have found, as he reflected on his experience, that the cheering and responsive supporters reinforced his sense of purpose and accomplishment. He wrote: "I am glad I made the late race. It gave me a hearing on the great and durable question of the age, which I could have had in no other way; and though I now sink out of view, and shall be forgotten, I believe I have made some marks which will tell for the cause of civil liberty long after I am gone."[28] As time has revealed, he was certainly not destined to "sink out of view."

1859

His loss to Douglas left Lincoln for a time in a political void, unsure what to do next. What was his "little engine" doing? He could not very well contest in 1860 the Senate seat of his ally, Lyman Trumbull, and

26. Schurz, "Reminiscences," 253.
27. Miers (ed.), *Lincoln Day By Day*, II, 230.
28. Noah Brooks, "The Life of Lincoln," in Arthur B. Lapsley (ed.), *The Writing of Abraham Lincoln* (8 vols.; New York, 1888), VIII, 170; Isaac N. Arnold, *A History of Abraham Lincoln* (Chicago, 1867), 122; Basler (ed.), *Collected Works*, III, 339.

Douglas' seat was safe until 1864. As yet, Lincoln's prospects for the presidency had not matured. Herndon, nevertheless, was insightful in his observation that Lincoln's "little engine" knew no rest.

During the ten months following his defeat, Lincoln returned full time to his law practice, attempting to recoup what he had spent in the 1858 contest. He was tempted to attend the Kansas State Republican Convention in May, but finally declined because too much time would have been required to get to the meeting place, Osawatomie. During August and September he turned down invitations to speak in Iowa, Minnesota, New York, Pennsylvania, and Wisconsin. These requests and other correspondence must have shown him that his debates had given him a nationwide following, but not until late in 1859 did Lincoln concede that he was a presidential possibility. In the last four months of 1859, he entered a new phase of his politicking, delivering eighteen or nineteen out-of-state speeches, which required about four thousand miles on the road.[29]

Without clearly defined personal goals that he would publicly admit, Lincoln resumed his attacks on Douglas' policies in order, he said, "to hedge against divisions in the Republican ranks." His out-of-state speaking started with an unplanned talk at Council Bluffs, Iowa, on August 13, while he was on a business trip to the western part of the state. The speech was of little significance; however, the request for it showed that Iowans were typical of many who were eager to see and hear Lincoln. Congenial, flexible, and ambitious, as always, he complied. In Iowa and elsewhere throughout the fall, he impressed his new friends by his simplicity and directness.[30]

Ohio. The Ohio Republicans provided Lincoln with a forum for attacking Douglas when they invited him to answer the Little Giant, who, joining the Ohio Democrats in the fall canvass, spoke at Columbus and Cincinnati. The time was fortunate for Lincoln; Douglas was receiving considerable coverage in the press for his article defending popular sovereignty—"The Dividing Line Between Federal and Local Authority"—which appeared in the September 9 issue of *Harper's Magazine.* The editor of the New York *Times,* Henry J.

29. Basler (ed.), *Collected Works,* III, 378; Stephen B. Oates, *Abraham Lincoln: The Man Behind the Myths* (New York, 1984), 75–77.

30. Abraham Lincoln to Schuyler Colfax, July 6, 1859, in Basler (ed.), *Collected Works,* III, 390; William Baringer, *Lincoln's Rise to Power* (Boston, 1937), 91–93.

Raymond, declared Douglas' Columbus speech to be the "opening manifesto of the Presidential canvass" and published its full text of 7,100 words.[31]

Having agreed to speak in Columbus and Cincinnati, Lincoln probably prepared two manuscripts. The opening speech, delivered on the terrace of the State House on September 16, was his "first careful, serious oration since the [1858] campaign." It appeared in full in the *Ohio State Journal* after Lincoln had carefully proofread it. His reception in Columbus was less enthusiastic than that afforded his opponent, and his audiences were smaller. He was, however, immediately pressed to make additional appearances, and that evening he spoke to the Young Republicans at City Hall. The following day, traveling the same rail route to Cincinnati that Douglas had taken, Lincoln appeared twice—for two hours between trains at Dayton and briefly at Hamilton. Arriving in Cincinnati late in the afternoon, Lincoln delivered his second prepared address at 8 P.M. to a mass meeting in Market Square. It was published in full in the Cincinnati *Gazette* and other Republican newspapers. After spending Sunday with Mrs. Lincoln's cousin, Lincoln stopped on the way home at Indianapolis for another two-hour speech. The invitation for it had come only the day before. In three days Lincoln had made six speeches. Two of these he later selected as major campaign documents and included in a volume of the Lincoln-Douglas debates published by the Ohio Republicans. It became a kind of primer for Republican orators and an important source for those who wanted to know more about Lincoln. On the Ohio trip he had demonstrated that his "little engine" was back on track and that he had widened his constituency.[32]

Wisconsin. Lincoln's reason for going to Wisconsin is less clear than that which prompted his Ohio trip. When the Wisconsin Agricultural Society invited him to deliver its annual address at the Wisconsin State Fair on September 30, Lincoln responded that he "had no address of the sort prepared; and could scarcely spare the time to prepare one," but he promised an answer by September 1. What moved him at this busy time to write a lecture on the place of labor in the American economic system, a subject far from his usual interests,

31. New York *Times*, September 8, 1858.

32. Basler (ed.), *Collected Works*, III, 400; Daniel J. Ryan, "Lincoln and Ohio," *Ohio Archaeological and Historical Publications*, XXXII (1923), 33–101.

remains a mystery. Always intrigued with lecturing, Lincoln saw in this invitation another opportunity to try his hand at this genre in which he had not been particularly successful. His acceptance of the invitation did not seem to have obvious political implications beyond allowing him an opportunity to make new friends.

After reaching Milwaukee, Lincoln added three extemporaneous political speeches to his schedule. Welcoming exposure, he may have hoped all along for such requests. The evening following his state fair lecture he talked at Newhall House, and though Wisconsin newspapers gave him valuable coverage, no report of this talk has survived. The next afternoon, following a long buggy ride, he spoke for two hours at Beloit and again in the evening in Janesville. In southeastern Wisconsin, Lincoln encountered listeners who, like those in Iowa and Ohio, wanted to hear his political views.[33]

Kansas. On a third trip outside Illinois, Lincoln made an eight-day circuit of frontier Kansas in December, probably because he wanted to visit the region and the people who had stirred so much controversy. He may also have hoped to give support to local Republicans in the coming December 6 election. His friend Mark W. Delahay, of Leavenworth, and Daniel W. Wilder, editor of the Elwood, Kansas, *Free Press*, had convinced Lincoln to brave winter travel for two scheduled major speeches. Journeying by rail from Springfield to Quincy, and from there taking the Hannibal and Saint Joseph Railroad to Saint Joseph, Missouri (over 206 miles), Lincoln spent the night of December 1 at Elwood, where the local Republicans persuaded him to favor them with an impromptu talk in the dining room of the Great Western Hotel. The following day, in bitter cold, Lincoln started out by open buggy pulled by one horse over primitive roads. Eight miles west, "blue with cold," he paused at Troy to speak to about forty people for an hour and three-quarters. He continued to Doniphan, about ten miles south, for a short impromptu talk, and closed out the day with a two-hour-and-twenty-minute speech at 8 P.M. in the Methodist church in Atchison, seven miles south of Doniphan. The next day he pressed on to Leavenworth (about twenty miles downriver), where upon his arrival he responded briefly to a formal welcome and that evening at Stockton Hall delivered his second

33. Basler (ed.), *Collected Works*, III, 397, 471–86; Louis W. Bridgman, *Lincoln Visits Beloit and Janesville, Wisconsin* (Madison, Wis., 1949), 1–14.

planned major address. After resting Sunday, December 5, he made, because of "insistent demands," his seventh speech since leaving Saint Joseph. He remained in Leavenworth through election day and probably returned upriver by steamer to Saint Joseph and from there by railroad back to Springfield on December 8. In Kansas, Lincoln most likely tried out some ideas that he intended to include in his Cooper Union speech, which he had known about since early October. He may have reasoned that this remote territory, away from the coverage of eastern newspapers, was a good place to test what he was planning for New York.[34]

An overview of his 1859 speaking suggests that Lincoln had advanced into another phase of his rhetorical career, broadening his efforts to reach audiences outside his home territory. Between 1854 and 1859 he had made only three speeches outside Illinois, but in 1859 he spoke in Iowa, Ohio, Wisconsin, and Kansas. In his home district, he attempted to aid in the congressional campaign of John M. Palmer, speaking impromptu on three occasions. In the spring he presented the lecture "Discoveries and Inventions" three times (in Jacksonville, Springfield, and Decatur). All the other appearances were "entirely unpremeditated." His public utterances of the year, including informal responses such as those to toasts and serenades, totaled only twenty-eight.[35]

1860

When did Lincoln rev up his "little engine" for the 1860 presidential campaign? During much of 1859, Lincoln refused to take seriously gossip about him as a contender in the 1860 presidential race. In his correspondence he showed concern about the success of the Republican party and its candidates and freely advised party strategists. After procrastinating about what move to make, on December 20 he yielded to pressure from his friend Jesse Fell, of Bloomington, and prepared what Lincoln dismissed as "a little sketch" but which enabled easterners to become familiar with him. With his characteristic humility, he said, "There is not much of it, for the reason that there is not much of me."[36]

---

34. Charles Arthur Hawley, "Lincoln in Kansas," *Illinois State Historical Journal*, XLII (1949), 179–92.

35. Basler (ed.), *Collected Works*, III, 484.

36. *Ibid.*, III, 511–12.

Cooper Union. Lincoln's political rhetoric reached its summit when he spoke at Cooper Union in New York City on February 27. At that time there could be little doubt about his "little engine," for he went east to impress eastern Republicans. The attack on Douglas that he had started in Springfield six years earlier now "reached its final development." For six years he had hammered away at his distinguished adversary, and out on the road he had conceived, developed, tested, and refined his arguments, a process clearly shown in his printed speeches. He knew that the New York audience demanded more than the customary political rhetoric extemporized and fashioned on the stump. Before western listeners, he had built his case against Douglas on circumstantial evidence and implications of guilt by association, evident in his oft repeated charge of conspiracy "between Stephen [Douglas], Franklin [Pierce], Roger [Taney], and James [Buchanan]" to nationalize slavery. But for his eastern listeners, he worked for weeks in the state library, reading Jonathan Elliot's *Debates in the Several State Conventions on the Adoption of the Federal Constitution*, the *Annals of Congress*, and the *Congressional Globe* in order to marshal facts to prove his case that the Founding Fathers expected the demise of slavery. Never before had Lincoln toiled so diligently on a political speech. Herndon reports, "It was constructed with a view of accuracy of statement, simplicity of language, and unity of thought. . . . No former effort in the line of speech-making had cost Lincoln so much time and thought as this one."[37]

Before leaving for New York on February 23, Lincoln bought a new suit in order to please his wife and make a good impression. He thought that he was going east to deliver a lecture for two hundred dollars at Beecher's Plymouth Church in Brooklyn, and only after his arrival on February 25 did he learn that the sponsorship had been transferred to the Young Men's Central Republican Union and the place shifted to Cooper Union. Taking over, the professional Republican managers advertised that the lecture was to be a "vindication of Republicanism." In response, fifteen hundred people, each willing to pay twenty-five cents, came to see and hear the westerner who had met the Little Giant on such equal terms.[38]

---

37. Angle, "Power With Words," 79; Basler (ed.), *Collected Works*, II, 465, 539; Herndon and Weik, *Life of Lincoln*, 367–68.

38. Abraham Lincoln to Cornelius F. McNeill, April 6, 1860, in Basler (ed.), *Collected Works*, IV, 38; Telegram from James A. Briggs to Lincoln, and Charles C. Nolt to Lincoln,

Lincoln knew that the speech was important. His consenting to deliver a lecture for a fee may lead one to question his objectives. Some have said that his primary purpose was simply to earn money to pay for a trip to see his son, who was in school in New Hampshire. Years after Lincoln's death, Herndon credited himself with advising Lincoln "to go by all means and to lecture on politics." Herndon continued, "I told Mr. Lincoln I thought it would help open the way to the Presidency." That Lincoln was planning ahead when he took such care in his speech preparation—more so than ever before—cannot be denied; but when he left Springfield, he did not know that the Republican managers had transformed his appearance into a media event. Once he arrived in New York and learned of the change in sponsorship, Lincoln further revised his manuscript.[39]

Lincoln, known for his frontier stumping, stirred the curiosity of many sophisticated easterners. They wondered what kind of antics they could expect from this self-educated lawyer and how this odd man would stand up in comparison to the dapper Douglas. When he rose to speak, he confirmed what they had probably anticipated; even his supporters were embarrassed. "His clothes were black and ill-fitting, badly wrinkled—as if they had been jammed carelessly into a small trunk. His bushy head, with the stiff black hair thrown back, was balanced on a long and lean head-stalk, and when he raised his hands in an opening gesture, I noticed that they were very large. He began in a low tone of voice—as if he were used to speaking out-doors and was afraid of speaking too loud. He said 'Mr. Cheerman,' instead of 'Mr. Chairman,' and employed many other words with an old-fashioned pronunciation."

But, as the speech unfolded, he took control of his listeners. "He straightened up, made regular and graceful gestures; his face lighted as with an inward fire; the whole man was transfigured. . . . When he reached a climax, the thunders of applause were terrific."[40]

October 12, 1859, both in David C. Mearns, *Lincoln Papers* (2 vols.; Garden City, N.Y., 1948), I, 227, 229.

39. William Herndon to Ward Lamon, March 6, 1870, in Emanuel Hertz, *The Hidden Lincoln: From the Letters and Papers of William H. Herndon* (New York, 1940), 76; "Recollection of McCormick," in Rufus Rockwell Wilson, *Intimate Memories of Lincoln* (Elmira, N.Y., 1945), 250; John G. Nicolay and John Hay, *Abraham Lincoln: A History* (10 vols.; New York, 1904), II, 41.

40. Brooks, "Life of Lincoln," in Lapsley (ed.), *The Writing of Abraham Lincoln*, VIII, 186–87.

New England. After a gracious reception in New York City, Lincoln set out for Exeter, New Hampshire, on the day after the Cooper Union speech, to visit his son at Phillips Exeter Academy. While in New York City, Lincoln learned that he was scheduled to deliver nine or ten speeches with the avowed purpose of aiding Republican candidates in Connecticut, Rhode Island, and New Hampshire, who were facing stiff competition in the coming elections. Although unaware of these appearances before leaving Springfield, he must have surmised and hoped that such invitations would be forthcoming. Concerned about the impression that he made, and mindful of the press coverage of the Cooper Union address, Lincoln wrote his wife: "The speech at New York, being within my calculation before I started, went off passably well and gave me no trouble whatever. The difficulty was to make nine others, before reading audiences who had already seen all my ideas in print."[41]

Still agreeable and politic, Lincoln coped with an exhausting schedule not too different from those of his Illinois campaigns. Constantly on the move, he responded enthusiastically to the cordiality of eager supporters and adjusted to changes in his plans. En route to Exeter he stopped at Providence, Rhode Island, on February 28 for his first speech. Once in Exeter, on March 1, he immediately took off on a side trip to speak at Concord at 11:45 A.M. and again in the evening at Manchester. An eyewitness gave a picture of Lincoln at this time. "Mr. Lincoln's oratory is natural and unstudied, which makes it more effective, and he possesses rare powers to elucidate and convince. Such a man must be heard to know his power." The following day he returned to Exeter and from there went to Dover for a speech scheduled after he had arrived in New Hampshire. On March 3 he addressed an audience in Exeter that included his son and his son's schoolmates. While in New Hampshire, Lincoln spoke to a total of five thousand or six thousand people. After visiting with his son over Sunday, he started back to New York, speaking every day from March 5 through 10—in Hartford; New Haven; Meriden; Woonsocket, Rhode Island; Norwich; and finally Bridgeport. In ten days he had made eleven 2-hour addresses.[42]

41. Abraham Lincoln to Isaac Pomeroy, March 3, 1860, Lincoln to Mary Todd Lincoln, March 4, 1860, both in Basler (ed.), *Collected Works*, III, 554–55.
42. Manchester (Vt.) *Daily American*, quoted in Edwin Page, *Abraham Lincoln in New Hampshire* (Boston, 1929), 53; Miers (ed.), *Lincoln Day by Day*, II, 273–75.

Following his arrival in New York, he was accepted as a celebrity, with supporters vying for his attention and prominent leaders entertaining him. No longer in the shadow of Douglas, Abraham Lincoln had become an important force in his party, with a greater part yet to come. The stump speaker who had perfected his rhetorical skills at crossroads and in rural villages of the West had demonstrated that even before sophisticated eastern listeners he could make a powerful speech.

The 175 speeches that he delivered between 1854 and 1860 give a good view of Lincoln, the political speaker, who sandwiched his campaigning into a busy law practice. The stump speaker Lincoln of the 1850s was aggressive; he kept his "little engine" running—usually at high speed—in contrast to the reluctant figure of the presidential years. "Following along," Lincoln stretched himself to meet the onslaught of his vigorous rival Douglas, always resourceful, wily, and persuasive. It was the Little Giant who took the lead, set the agenda, often attracted the crowd, and put Lincoln in a posture to gain national notice. Lincoln was pleased to give "concluding speeches" to Douglas' representation of popular sovereignty. Reporters, eager to write about the newsworthy Douglas, could not ignore his ever-present opponent.

Lincoln was an indefatigable campaigner, stumping day after day and enduring various discomforts. There is no record that he ever lost his temper, scolded the local arrangement committees, or responded in kind to the pettiness or vindictiveness of opponents. In dress and manner he continued to project the image of Old Abe—"colloquial, affable, good natured, almost jolly"—a simple, honest person. When a friend asked him why, in speaking against Douglas, he did not use anecdotes, Lincoln replied that "he thought the occasion was too grave and serious. He said that the principal complaint he had to make against Mr. Douglas was his continual assumption of superiority on account of his elevated position." True to these feelings, a sober Lincoln concentrated on issues, not personalities, keeping his humor subtle and ironic, and his arguments legalistic and historical. Throughout these busy times, Lincoln kept abreast of his subject by daily reading of the newspapers and the *Congressional Globe*.[43]

Whether Lincoln used speaker's notes is not known, but he must have always carried along pertinent clippings and copies of his and

43. New York *Tribune*, June 26, 1858; Hertz, *Hidden Lincoln*, 288.

Douglas' recent speeches. Remaining fragments in his collected papers suggest that he crystallized his thinking by writing out segments on vital topics, but he altered these passages when he fitted them into his development. He did use manuscripts for his lectures, for the House Divided speech, perhaps for the Columbus and Cincinnati speeches, and for the Cooper Union address; but blessed with an excellent memory, he never held himself to his prepared manuscript.[44]

During the six pre-presidential years, Lincoln, a one-issue man, never gave up on opposing the extension of slavery in the territories. In spite of being placed on the defensive for such statements as "this government cannot endure permanently half-slave and half-free," he never retreated from his central message.

Lincoln sometimes had to walk a fine line, denying over and over that he was an abolitionist and refusing to be closely associated with radical elements of his party. On numerous platforms, he insisted without equivocation that slavery was morally wrong, but he averred that he would not disturb "the peculiar institution" where it was constitutionally protected. By his rhetorical skill he kept himself well in the middle, a position that eventually made him attractive as a presidential candidate.

During his campaigns, Lincoln did not always make his goals public. He wanted a United States Senate seat and a strong Republican party, but he was cautious about declaring ultimate objectives. When did he direct his "little engine" toward the presidency? Certainly not during his debates with Douglas; he did not let his personal ambitions go that far. In the role of a good party man, he wished to force Douglas into some awkward positions, because weakening his rival as a presidential candidate was a good way to promote any Republican nominee. Not until the late fall of 1859 did Lincoln show signs of hoping for the nomination himself. The image of following along after Douglas stayed with him until Cooper Union. Only with that appearance did Lincoln take center stage.

44. Joseph Gillespie to Jesse Weik, January 31, 1866, in Hertz, *Hidden Lincoln*, 288.

III

"KINDLY LET ME BE SILENT"
A Reluctant Lincoln

Historians and biographers praise Abraham Lincoln for his two inaugural speeches and the Gettysburg Address, but they are likely to say little about the remainder of his presidential speaking. Because the three masterpieces were well prepared and polished in manuscript and because emphasis is often placed on his letters and state papers, which constitute accessible source material, some critics conclude that he was primarily a writer and therefore dismiss his speaking as unimportant.[1] As president, Lincoln could not avoid speaking (though he attempted to), and his rhetorical strategy and total oral output, including day-by-day impromptu and extemporaneous utterances, provide insight into how he functioned while in office. It is appropriate, therefore, to consider Lincoln's presidential speaking from the time of his nomination until his assassination.

Lincoln's rhetorical stance after his nomination in 1860 was considerably different from that during his campaigning, so much so that one writer called the "hiatus . . . baffling."[2] His change in tone and mood becomes evident when his pre- and post-nomination speaking is compared. Prior to May, 1860, Lincoln was eager to speak, seldom refused invitations to rallies, and enjoyed give-and-take of the hustings. In each campaign he was out on the stump promoting his party and its candidates and, when he was seeking office, himself. This was the Lincoln that Douglas declared "the strong man of his party—full of wit, facts, dates, and the best stump-speaker with droll-ways and dry jokes in the west."[3] After 1854 he became more serious about his rhetorical art, concentrated his opposition to the extension of slavery in the territories, denounced both the repeal of the Missouri Compro-

1. Herbert Joseph Edwards and John Erskine Hankins, "Lincoln the Writer: The Development of His Literary Style," *University of Maine Bulletin*, LXIV (April 10, 1962), 80–81; T. Harry Williams (ed.), *Selected Writings and Speeches of Abraham Lincoln* (Chicago, 1943), xviii–liii; Luther Emerson Robinson, *Abraham Lincoln as a Man of Letters* (Chicago, 1918), 9.
2. Byron D. Murray, "Lincoln Speaks," *Contemporary Review*, CVIII (May, 1966), 250.
3. John W. Forney, *Anecdotes of Public Men* (2 vols.; New York, 1881), II, 179.

mise and popular sovereignty, and made Senator Stephen A. Douglas his principal target. In the presidential canvass of 1856, he spoke probably fifty times, and during his 1858 bid for Douglas' Senate seat, he addressed over sixty audiences in a four-month period.

After his nomination for the presidency, Lincoln altered his rhetorical strategy. He became a reluctant speaker, cautious about what he said, never again to campaign, and seldom to advance "doctrinal points" in a speech. Consistent with the customary practice of presidential candidates, he let surrogates speak for him in 1860 and refused to discuss personally the party platform or to amplify his position on current issues. Lincoln's reluctance to appear on the public platform was in direct contrast to the willingness of Douglas, who toured extensively in the East, Middle West, and South.

Repeatedly Lincoln reaffirmed his determination to remain silent. In a June 19, 1860, letter to Samuel Galloway, he wrote, "In my present position . . . by the lessons of the past, and the united voice of all discreet friends, I am neither [to] write or speak a word for the public." Urged to respond at a Republican rally in Springfield on August 8, 1860, he told the hometown audience that he had come "with no intention of making a speech. It has been my purpose, since I have been placed in my present position [the nomination], to make no speeches." In concluding, he requested, "Kindly let me be silent." A few days later, Lincoln refused to "write or speak anything upon doctrinal points," claiming that his "published speeches contain nearly all I could willingly say." When William S. Speer of Shelbyville, Tennessee, pressed Lincoln on October 13, 1860, to "disclaim" in writing "all intention to interfere with slaves or slavery in the States," Lincoln replied: "It would do no good. I have already done this many times; and it is in print, and open to all who will read. Those who will not read, or heed, what I have already publicly said, would not read, or heed, a repetition of it. 'If they hear not Moses and the prophets, neither will they be persuaded though one rose from the dead.'"[4]

In the canvass Lincoln had good reason for standing firm on what he had previously said. He was aware that he had won the nomination because he was not an extremist and that his conservatism represented

<hr>

4. Roy P. Basler (ed.), *The Collected Works of Abraham Lincoln* (9 vols.; New Brunswick, N.J., 1953), IV, 80, 91, 93, 130.

a middle ground within a wide spectrum of opinions, including those of abolitionists, German-Americans, and former Whigs and Know-Nothings. In spite of attempts to pull him off center, he kept as his main appeal his opposition to the extension of slavery in the territories. He attempted to avoid taking positions that might alienate any of his diverse supporters in the North and in the border states as well as old-time Whigs throughout the South.

After the election, Lincoln continued to hold his silence. On November 21, 1860, when his train stopped at Lincoln, Illinois, en route to Chicago, he told his assembled admirers, "I am not in the habit of making speeches now, and I would therefore ask to be excused from entering upon any discussion of the political topics of the day."[5]

Lincoln's reluctance to speak on substantive issues was much in evidence during his twelve-day trip to Washington (February 11 to February 23) for his inauguration. Although he made numerous stops along the circuitous route, greeted thousands of curious onlookers, and delivered at least ninety-four speeches—sometimes as many as twelve a day—he remained silent about the developing events and what measures he had in mind to meet the sectional crisis. He kept his comments general, speaking mainly at ovations, public receptions, and other festivities as he passed through the capitals in the states critical to the Republican victory: Indiana, Ohio, New York, New Jersey, and Pennsylvania.

On the first day of the journey, replying to the welcome of Governor Oliver P. Morton of Indiana, Lincoln declared his rhetorical approach to the trip. "I do not expect upon this occasion or any occasion till I get to Washington to attempt any lengthy speech." On the whole, Lincoln adhered to this plan, delivering no more than a sentence or two at a whistle-stop and frequently rephrasing what he had said previously. In spite of fatigue, he remained cordial and accommodating, reasserting his determination to abide by the Constitution and maintain the Union. He minimized the crisis, calling it "an artificial one," and avoided being maneuvered into making careless statements about policy.[6]

Lincoln wished "to make no mistake before taking further bearings" and to defer "difficult public questions for appropriate and mature

5. *Ibid.*, IV, 143.
6. *Ibid.*, IV, 193, 211.

treatment in the coming inaugural." Faced with rumors of threats to his life and schemes to thwart his inauguration, he chose to appear noncontroversial and uncommitted to specific policies until his new administration was in place. He hoped to delay further erosion of the Union and perhaps to give the seceders time to make a provocative threat that would justify overt action by the federal government.[7]

Lincoln demonstrated his ability to suggest possible actions without committing himself when he reflected on the meaning of the terms *coercion* and *invasion* in a carefully conceived speech.

The words "coercion" and "invasion" are in great use about these days. Suppose we were simply to try if we can, and ascertain what, is the meaning of these words. Let us get, if we can, the exact definitions of these words—not from dictionaries, but from the men who constantly repeat them—what things they mean to express by the words. What, then, is "coercion"? What is "invasion"? Would the marching of an army into South Carolina, for instance, without the consent of her people, and in hostility against them, be coercion or invasion? I very frankly say, I think it would be invasion, and it would be coercion too, if the people of that country were forced to submit. But if the Government, for instance, but simply insists upon holding its own forts, or retaking those forts which belong to it, or the enforcement of the laws of the United States in the collection of duties upon foreign importations, or even the withdrawal of the mails from those portions of the country where the mails themselves are habitually violated; would any or all of these things be coercion? Do the lovers of the Union contend that they will resist coercion or invasion of any State, understanding that any or all of these would be coercing or invading a State? If they do, then it occurs to me that the means for the preservation of the Union they so greatly love, in their own estimation, is of a very thin and airy character. If sick, they would consider the little pills of the homoepathist as already too large for them to swallow. In their view, the Union, as a family relation, would not be anything like a regular marriage at all, but only as a sort of free-love arrangement, to be maintained on what that sect calls passionate attraction.[8]

In Cincinnati he told two thousand German workers eager to know how he planned to meet the crisis, "I deem it my duty that I should wait until the last moment, for a development of the present national difficulties, before I express myself decidedly what course I shall pursue." In Pittsburgh, Lincoln continued to express his hesitancy. "It is naturally expected that I should say something upon this subject, but to touch upon it at all would involve an elaborate discussion of a

7. James G. Randall, *Lincoln, the President* (4 vols.; New York, 1945–55), I, 279.
8. Basler (ed.), *Collected Works*, IV, 195.

great many questions and circumstances, would require more time than I can at present command, and would perhaps unnecessarily commit me upon matters which have not yet fully developed themselves."[9]

In two speeches, Lincoln took care to be conciliatory and to express goodwill toward southerners. In Cincinnati he directed his comments to neighboring Kentuckians, reassuring them that he intended to leave them alone and "in no way interfere with [their] institutions." In the previously mentioned address in Pittsburgh, referring to "the troubles across the river," he suggested, "If the great American people will only keep their temper, on both sides of the line, the troubles will come to an end, and the question which now distracts the country will be settled."[10]

At hurried brief stops, Lincoln greeted crowds with such remarks as "I have no time for long speeches, and could not make them at every place without wearing myself out" or "I regret I cannot stop to speak to you" or "I have no speech to make, and no sufficient time to make one." In New York City, near the end of the harrying trip, after being constantly entertained and displayed, and after greeting, conferring with, and interviewing many people, Lincoln reiterated his rhetorical strategy. "I have been occupying a position since the Presidential election, of silence, of avoiding public speaking, of avoiding public writing."[11]

There is truth in the judgment that "nothing could have been more banal and indifferent" than most of these speeches. With the exception of Lincoln's eloquent little farewell address at Springfield, these utterances are seldom quoted, and though he did show deep feelings when he spoke at Independence Hall, none represent memorable oratory. He gave greater consideration to what he said before state legislatures and in large cities than at railroad junctions and cross-roads. Nevertheless, when the ninety-four speeches are judged for their rhetorical purpose, they demonstrate that Lincoln was successful at playing out his waiting game.[12]

In *The Collected Works of Abraham Lincoln*, Roy P. Basler groups Lincoln's oral efforts under five headings: remarks, responses, replies, speeches, and addresses. Some of these items may not have been

9. *Ibid.*, IV, 202, 210.
10. *Ibid.*, IV, 199, 211.
11. *Ibid.*, IV, 217, 220, 223, 230.
12. Clarence Edward Macartney, *Lincoln and His Cabinet* (New York, 1931), 11.

public speeches in the usual sense of the term, and they do not include annual messages to Congress (forwarded to be read by someone else) or other state papers that have a rhetorical flavor. Many of the ninety-five items were impromptu, a minute or two in length, delivered at serenades, at public ceremonies, or to military units passing through Washington. Some were responses (perhaps suggested by the secretary of state and often made in his presence) to diplomats or to small groups bringing petitions or gifts. These little speeches usually appeared in the third person in newspaper articles and were often paraphrased by the reporter.[13]

From 1860 onward, Lincoln prepared few complete manuscripts. Extant copies include his two inaugural addresses; the GettysburgAddress; a plea delivered July 12, 1862, to representatives of the border states to accept a plan of compensated emancipation; and his last public address, to serenaders, on reconstruction, delivered April 9, 1865, following Robert E. Lee's surrender at Appomattox. Lincoln confined his speeches mainly to ceremonies associated with his high office and having little to do with policy matters.

In his three major presidential addresses, well spaced throughout his four years, carefully prepared and delivered with manuscript in hand, Lincoln demonstrated sensitivity to rhetorical detail and modesty about his prominent position. Each presentation grew out of events of the moment, which dictated his choice of topics.

His First Inaugural Address, in preparation for more than a month and reviewed by trusted advisers, was a policy statement in which Lincoln sought to answer questions that the public had impatiently pressed upon him since his nomination. Using a legalistic, almost emotionless approach, Lincoln responded in a conciliatory spirit to the crisis fomented by the recent secession of the states of the lower South. Remaining consistent with his pre-inaugural statements, he announced that he would abide strictly by the Constitution and the Republican platform, carry out the obligation of his oath of office, and not disturb domestic institutions such as slavery within the states (force no "obnoxious strangers among the people" in rebellion). He said, "There needs to be no bloodshed or violence unless it be forced upon the national authority." But Lincoln showed no timidity about calling secession "insurrectionary or revolutionary" or about his plan

13. Earl Schenck Miers (ed.), *Lincoln Day by Day: A Chronology, 1809–1865* (3 vols.; Washington, D.C., 1960), III, 123, 143–44, 221, 253, 265.

to protect federal property. "In *your* hands, my dissatisfied fellow-countrymen, not in *mine*, is the momentous issue of civil war. The government will not assail *you*. You can have no conflict without being yourselves the aggressors. *You* have no oath registered in heaven to destroy the government, while *I* shall have the most solemn one to 'preserve, protect, and defend' it."[14]

Lincoln thus shut the door on compromise and shifted the onus of aggression to the seceders. Projecting a relaxed attitude, he counseled patience to await further developments. Some interpreted his mood as conciliatory, and some as indecisive. Southerners, well along in their plans to move against federal properties, called the address a declaration of war; others saw it as a play for time to mobilize.[15]

No better example of Lincoln's reluctance as a speaker can be found than in his attitude toward delivering the Gettysburg Address. He raised no objections to presenting a two-minute addendum to Edward Everett's carefully prepared address, which strove for a grandeur fitting to the event. Lincoln's secondary role caused him no ill feelings. In his "few appropriate remarks," just ten sentences, Lincoln, as usual, engaged in self-depreciation. Shifting attention from his position and from the formalities of the day, he observed, "The world will little note, nor long remember what we say here, but it can never forget what they [the brave men] did here." He could not know how wrong he was about the permanence of his words. The sober, meditative Lincoln both by mood and word expressed contriteness, selflessness, and good taste—without oratorical flourish or pomposity. This reserve was his way of giving full respect to the "honored dead" and to the ideal of freedom.

Of the Second Inaugural Address, Carl Sandburg wrote, "Seldom had a President been so short-spoken about the issues of so grave an hour." Lincoln seemed almost embarrassed to take time for a second inaugural address; hence, it was one of the shortest inaugural speeches that had ever been given. He avoided any waving of the bloody shirt and exuberance about military successes, suggesting only that the "progress of our arms . . . is as well known to the public as to myself and . . . is reasonably satisfactory and satisfactory to all." With victory at hand, Lincoln "ventured . . . no predictions" about the future.

14. Basler (ed.), *Collected Works*, IV, 271.
15. Carl Sandburg, *Abraham Lincoln: The Prairie Years and the War Years* (New York, 1954), 214–15.

Hesitant to assess blame for the war—"judge not that we not be judged"—Lincoln put its outcome in God's hands. The phrase "With malice toward none, with Charity for all" embodies the great magnanimity of Lincoln.[16]

Lincoln's three masterpieces reflect what he said about the eloquence of Henry Clay—that it consisted "of deeply earnest and impassioned tone, and manner, which can proceed only from great sincerity and a thorough conviction in the speaker of the justice and importance of his cause. This it is, that truly touches the chords of human sympathy. . . . All his efforts were made for practical effect. He never spoke merely to be heard."[17]

The First Inaugural Address was one of Lincoln's longest after 1860, consisting of about 3,700 words, but the Gettysburg Address, which took less than two minutes to deliver, was only 270 words long, and the Second Inaugural Address comprised 700 words and was probably read in six to seven minutes. Adept at rationalizing both his brevity and his unwillingness to commit himself, Lincoln explained his reticence in one of four ways: he had nothing to say; he was not prepared; someone else was more deserving of being heard; or, as president, it was "not becoming" for him to respond. To serenaders celebrating the victory at Gettysburg, Lincoln said, "This is a glorious theme and occasion for a speech, but I am not prepared to make one worthy of the occasion." On the eve of the Gettysburg Address, when an enthusiastic crowd beckoned him from his lodging, Lincoln simply explained, "I have no speech to make." And on July 4, 1861, when addressing a New York regiment, he good-naturedly said: "I appear before you in obedience to your call; not however, to make a speech. I have made a great many poor speeches in my life, and I feel considerably relieved now to know that the dignity of the position in which I have been placed does not permit me to expose myself longer. I therefore take shelter, most gladly in standing back and allowing you to hear speeches from gentlemen who are so very much more able to make them than myself."[18]

On a rare instance when he appeared at a public rally, on August 6, 1862, Lincoln for once almost forgot his reserve. Stirred by a resolution and regretting "a want of readiness and determination" on the part

16. *Ibid.*, 663; Basler (ed.), *Collected Works*, VIII, 333.
17. Basler (ed.), *Collected Works*, II, 127.
18. *Ibid.*, VI, 320; VII, 17; IV, 441.

of those directing the Union's military operations, Lincoln, perhaps impulsively, defended General George B. McClellan and Secretary of War Edwin M. Stanton. Giving his remarks a little bite, Lincoln told the gathering, "I however have an impression that there are younger gentlemen who will entertain you better and better address your understanding, than I will or could and therefore I propose but to detain you a moment longer." After his rejoinder, he concluded, "I have talked longer than I expected to do and now I avail myself of my privilege of saying no more."[19]

At a tense time when northern sentiment was stirred over a rumor that Confederate forces had massacred a regiment of black troops at Fort Pillow, Tennessee, Lincoln said, at the Sanitary Fair in Baltimore on April 18, 1864, "It is not very becoming for one in my position to make speeches at great length; but there is another subject upon which I feel that I ought to say a word." He then explained that the incident was to be thoroughly investigated.[20]

Lincoln often suggested that it was unwise for him, as president, to comment. He was always keenly aware of his responsibilities as the spokesman for his administration and of the possibility that some reporters might misinterpret or misrepresent a careless remark. In October, 1862, during a tour of Maryland, he reflected that it was "hardly proper" for him to make speeches because "every word is so closely noted that it will not do to make trivial ones." When negotiations were in progress for Lee's surrender, Lincoln again showed caution. "Everything I say, you know, goes into print. If I make a mistake it doesn't merely affect me nor you, but the country. I therefore ought at least try not to make mistakes."[21]

Because of his reticence, Lincoln seldom ventured beyond Washington on speaking trips. He delivered seventy-eight of his ninety-five presidential speeches at the White House—in his office, in a reception room, or from a window or balcony. Seven talks were made elsewhere within the city. When he traveled beyond the capital, visiting the armies to confer with his generals, he attempted to attract as little attention as possible and never made speeches. Lincoln made only ten addresses (some very brief) outside Washington: one on June 24, 1862, in Jersey City while en route to West Point; two on October

19. *Ibid.*, V, 358.
20. *Ibid.*, VII, 302.
21. *Ibid.*, V, 450; VII, 394; IV, 220.

4, 1862, at Frederick, Maryland; two on a three-day trip to Gettysburg; one on April 18, 1864, at the Sanitary Commission Fair in Baltimore; and four on June 16, 1864, at the Central Sanitary Fair in Philadelphia. At a banquet held during the Philadelphia fair, Lincoln responded to a toast by observing that the event "was intended to open the way for me to say something." He explained, "I did not know, but that I might be called upon to say a few words before I got away from here, but I did not know it was coming just here." Many political figures at such a moment would have resorted to an oratorical flourish, but not Lincoln. After he had praised the Sanitary Commission for its activities, he shifted attention to the prospect of General Ulysses S. Grant's "pouring forward" in Virginia. The four brief speeches at the fair constituted an unusual amount of speaking for Lincoln.[22]

The rhetoric of a president usually reflects the aura of his office. If he is wise, he learns that as chief executive he no longer speaks only for himself or his party, but for his administration and for the nation as a whole. Responsibility weighs heavily upon him and powerfully influences his rhetorical choices. What he might previously have said casually to local supporters in the midst of the give-and-take of a campaign speech now becomes inappropriate and unwise, for the slightest slip or impropriety becomes grist for inquiring reporters and hostile editors. Constantly in the public eye, with the press always close at hand, a president must anticipate public reaction to a pronouncement. The resulting pressure explains why much presidential oratory is abstract, noncommittal, and even bland, in spite of the utilization of the best speech-writing talent available.

No better case study of the influence of the office on the presidential rhetoric exists than that of Abraham Lincoln. He packed his speaking into a busy schedule that did not allow time for reflection. Unlike twentieth-century presidents, he had no staff of speech writers, no stenographers on call to take shorthand, and no tape recorder. Never after his nomination in 1860 did he escape the tyranny of public scrutiny. During the 1860 canvass, he could not risk free expression because he feared alienating some of his diverse supporters. His preinaugural speaking was dampened by secession and rumors of plots to disrupt his taking office. The awesome tasks of maintaining unity in the North, holding the border states, and supporting the military

22. *Ibid.*, VII, 304.

operations forced upon Lincoln, inexperienced in administration, the necessity for caution, reserve, and at times silence.

The ultimate test of rhetorical choice is how it influences listeners, that is, how it achieves the speaker's persuasive goals. In the case of Lincoln, his reluctance was consistent with his humble man image of past days. In the presidential role, Lincoln did not change; he continued to portray himself as a modest, down-to-earth westerner who was struggling to do the best that he could in the face of a fearsome crisis.

IV

"A REMORSELESS ANALYZER"
Lincoln's Speech Preparation

When Abraham Lincoln said that all Henry Clay's speeches "were made for practical effect" and that "he never spoke merely to be heard," he could well have been commenting on his own rhetorical career. Busy in the courtroom, at political meetings and conventions, and later in the presidency, Lincoln never took time to explain his rhetorical theory or practice, or to pontificate on eloquence in general. The only way, therefore, to learn about his rhetorical habits is to study him in action and to read what little his contemporaries remembered about him.

Scholars have been plagued by the question "How knoweth this man letters, having never learned?" What seems remarkable is that in spite of frontier hardships, including a dearth of books, the self-taught Lincoln advanced far beyond the illiteracy typical of his day so evident in the letters and habits of his own relatives.

In his autobiography, Lincoln (referring to himself in the third person) recorded that after he was "twenty-three . . . he studied English grammar, imperfectly of course, but so as to speak and write as well as he now [in 1860] does." At best, his meager rhetorical resources included little more than Samuel Kirkham's *Grammar*, Thomas Dilworth's *New Guide to the English Tongue*, perhaps *The Kentucky Preceptor*, and William Scott's *Lessons on Elocution*; and "the aggregate of all his schooling did not amount to one year." In spite of his limited education, Lincoln rapidly developed a simple, direct, and at times eloquent style, mastered argumentative analysis, and became an effective persuader.[1]

What were his sources and models? Many of the people interviewed by William H. Herndon testified to Lincoln's intense interest in reading newspapers, lawbooks, and borrowed textbooks. He was greatly

---

1. Roy P. Basler (ed.), *The Collected Works of Abraham Lincoln* (9 vols.; New Brunswick, N.J., 1953), II, 126; IV, 62.

influenced by the Bible, adopting its imagery and rhythms. He enjoyed poetry, even trying his hand at it, and delighted in the works of Shakespeare, Robert Burns, and Oliver Wendell Holmes. Roy P. Basler suggests that Lincoln read the *Arabian Nights*, David Ramsay's *Life of Washington*, William Grimshaw's *History of the United States*, Aesop's *Fables*, Bunyan's *Pilgrim's Progress*, Defoe's *Robinson Crusoe*, and Parson Weems's *The Life and Memorable Actions of George Washington*. Nevertheless, Lincoln could not be said to have read widely, "comparatively speaking had no knowledge of literature," and, according to Herndon, had read "no histories, novels, biographies, etc." In spite of his efforts, Herndon could not interest his law partner in philosophical treatises and abolitionist literature. It was the younger man who was the bookworm in the Lincoln-Herndon office and who collected one of the better libraries in Springfield. Basler writes that "no other person contributed more to his [Lincoln's] intellectual development directly and indirectly than Herndon did through his perpetual reading and discussion of books."[2]

The reliability of Herndon's evaluations of Lincoln's reading is difficult to determine because he recorded his recollections long after Lincoln's death and tended to emphasize his own importance. Nevertheless, he had more opportunities than anyone else to observe the future president at close range, and there is little doubt that Lincoln profited from their conversations and from Herndon's books. In addition, Lincoln often sought his partner's opinions about political matters, particularly the activities of the abolitionists.[3]

Lincoln shaped his rhetoric according to the exacting requirements of the legal profession. Early in his career at New Salem, he borrowed lawbooks, studied the English jurist Sir William Blackstone, and drafted legal instruments for his neighbors. His second partner, Stephen T. Logan, who had a reputation as "a stickler for painstaking precision," had a positive influence on the young lawyer. On the circuit and at the hustings, Lincoln learned from observing judges, politicians, clergymen, and other lawyers, such as David Davis,

2. Emanuel Hertz (ed.), *The Hidden Lincoln: From the Letters and Papers of William H. Herndon* (New York, 1938), 424–29; William H. Herndon and Jesse W. Weik, *Herndon's Life of Lincoln* (New York, 1930), 258–59; Joseph Fort Newton, *Lincoln and Herndon* (Cedar Rapids, Iowa, 1910), 249–51; Roy P. Basler (ed.), *Abraham Lincoln: His Speeches and Writings* (Cleveland, 1946), 12.

3. David H. Donald, *Lincoln's Herndon* (New York, 1948), 303, 320.

Lyman Trumbull, Owen Lovejoy, Peter Cartwright, and Stephen Douglas. He broadened his perspectives at political conventions, before the Illinois legislature, and in the United States House of Representatives. He revered Henry Clay and had thoughtfully read some of Daniel Webster's speeches. [4]

How Lincoln conceived ideas and mastered a subject may indicate how he put a speech together. Fellow lawyer Henry Clay Whitney described Lincoln's mind as working "slowly like the ponderous ocean steamer engine." Herndon remembered that Lincoln's "perception [was] slow, cold, clear, and exact" and that he was "a remorseless analyzer of facts, things, and principles." Agreeing that Lincoln was a slow thinker, another close associate, James Cook Conkling, recalled that "every proposition submitted to his mind was subjected to the regular process of a syllogism, with its major proposition and its minor proposition and its conclusion. Whatever could not stand the test of sound reasoning, he rejected." [5]

Able to concentrate best when he was alone, Lincoln would slip away from his office to a quiet place, perhaps a vacant office or the state library. It is doubtful that he did much serious studying at home or at his law office. Colleagues on the circuit reported that he sometimes read late at night after others were asleep. His first two law partners, Logan and John T. Stuart, unfortunately tell little about their day-to-day associations with the young lawyer. One impression was that Lincoln was unsystematic and perhaps even careless in handling office details and that he was better in the courtroom than at his desk.

Comparatively little is reported about how Lincoln prepared his speeches prior to 1854. His two early published lectures, "The Perpetuation of Our Political Institutions" (1838) and the "Temperance Address" (1842), showed that he had commenced to master the rhetorical art. Aware of the young legislator's reputation as an orator, the Young Men's Lyceum and the Washington Temperance Society invited him to present formal lectures at public meetings. The care

4. John J. Duff, A. Lincoln: Prairie Lawyer (New York, 1960), 79; Stephen T. Logan, "Talks About Lincoln," Bulletin, Abraham Lincoln Association, Springfield, Illinois, No. 12 (September 1, 1928), 1–3; Richard N. Current, "Lincoln and Daniel Webster," Journal of the Illinois State Historical Society, XLVII (August, 1955), 307–21.
5. Henry Clay Whitney, Life on the Circuit with Lincoln (Caldwell, Idaho, 1940), 128; James Cook Conkling, "Early Bench and Bar of Central Illinois," in Rufus Rockwell Wilson (ed.), Lincoln Among His Friends (Caldwell, Idaho, 1942), 107.

that Lincoln took in analysis, organization, choice of language and composition showed that he was highly pleased by the recognition from fellow townsmen. It was even more satisfying to him to see the two manuscripts published and distributed throughout Springfield.[6]

In his campaigning between 1854 and 1859, Lincoln inductively assembled his constructive case, which opposed the extension of slavery in the territories. Few days passed during which he was not studying his position — reading, listening, rephrasing, refocusing, and strengthening his arguments, mainly aimed at Stephen Douglas. On the stump he was continually testing and refining his arguments — first, before the voters in Illinois; later, before those in Ohio, Wisconsin, and Kansas; and finally, at Cooper Union in New York City.

On October 4, 1854, in Springfield, Lincoln delivered his first major thrust against Douglas; this speech has survived only in a newspaper report. Twelve days later, in Peoria, Lincoln delivered practically the same talk, advancing the position from which he continued to argue through 1860. After delivering the Peoria speech, he wrote it out at the urging of supporters. Albert J. Beveridge, a Lincoln biographer and a noted speaker in his own right, took special interest in Lincoln's "uncommon thoroughness" in preparing this address. He wrote that "for weeks Lincoln had spent toilsome hours in the State Library, searching trustworthy histories, analyzing the Census, mastering the facts, reviewing the literature of the subject." Beveridge suggested that Lincoln had sharpened his thinking by ghostwriting editorials for Whig newspapers.[7]

THE HOUSE DIVIDED SPEECH

John G. Nicolay and John Hay, Lincoln's official biographers, suggest that the House Divided speech of June 16, 1858, delivered at the Republican state convention in Springfield "was perhaps the most carefully prepared speech of his [Lincoln's] whole life. Every word of it was written, every sentence had been tested. . . . It was not an ordinary oration." They may have overstated the case, but there is little doubt that Lincoln pondered the implications of what he put into his manuscript. He was "at it off and on about one month. If a good idea struck him . . . he penciled it down on a small slip of paper and put it in his hat where he carried quite all his plunder." Behind closed doors

6. Basler (ed.), *Collected Works*, I, 108–15, 271–79.
7. Albert J. Beveridge, *Abraham Lincoln, 1809–1858* (2 vols.; Boston, 1928), II, 238.

he read an early version to his partner and later to a dozen or so of his friends, including Jesse K. Dubois, James Cook Conkling, and James H. Matheny, in a room over the library of the State House. In spite of their contrary counsel, Lincoln remained determined to keep the speech as he had written it. Chicago reporter Horace White, who said it was the only speech he ever heard Lincoln read from manuscript, recalled, "After the convention adjourned he handed me his manuscript and asked me to read the proof of it at the office of the *Illinois State Journal* where it had already been put in type." Lincoln also stopped by the newspaper office to look over the revised proofs. According to White, Lincoln stressed that "he had taken a great deal of pains with his speech and that he wanted it to go before the people just as he had prepared it." Lincoln's eagerness to preserve a verbatim copy of the House Divided pronouncement suggests that he felt that it stated the point of contention between Douglas and him. On later occasions Lincoln read from the printed version to leave no doubt what he had said—and still believed. [8]

THE LINCOLN-DOUGLAS DEBATES

Many of the details of how Lincoln prepared for the senatorial campaign of 1858 were not recorded; however, he drew heavily upon what he had assembled for the two previous campaigns. An important part of his immediate preparation was to follow newspaper reports on Douglas' activities and statements and to listen intently to what the Little Giant said in Chicago (July 9) and Bloomington (July 16) and at places where their paths crossed during the canvass. After agreeing to the seven meetings, Lincoln remained in Springfield between July 29 and August 11 to reflect, answer his mail, read in the state library, and consult with advisers; in addition, he gathered clippings from available newspapers and read Herndon's scrapbook. "In his trips to and fro over the State, between meetings, he would stop at Springfield sometimes, to consult with his friends or to post himself up on questions that occurred during the canvass," reported Herndon. "He kept me busy hunting up old speeches and gathering facts and statistics at the State library. I made liberal clippings bearing in any way on the questions of the hour from every newspaper I happened to see, and

8. John G. Nicolay and John Hay, *Abraham Lincoln: A History* (10 vols.; New York, 1904), II, 136; Ward H. Lamon, *The Life of Abraham Lincoln from His Birth to His Inauguration as President* (Boston, 1872), 398; Horace White, Introduction, in William H. Herndon and Jesse W. Weik, *Abraham Lincoln: The True Story of a Great Life* (2 vols.; New York, 1892), II, 92.

kept him supplied with them; and on one or two occasions, in answer to letters and telegrams, I sent books forward to him."[9]

In spite of what Herndon implied, once Lincoln resumed active campaigning, he had little time for research in Springfield. Out on the road he continued to read newspaper reports about the Democrats and consulted with supporters who had heard Douglas. Much of the time he had the advantage of traveling and conversing with Horace White, who helped keep him abreast of Douglas' activities. On September 19, Lincoln paused in Winchester to read the *Congressional Globe* in the office of Judge John Moses. At crucial moments he discussed his strategy with Republican advisers, including Joseph Medill, E.B. Washburne, David Davis, and Norman Judd, but he did not always take their advice. Before the Freeport debate, for example, they warned him about one of the questions he intended to ask Douglas, but Lincoln persisted. Douglas' answer, which stated that in spite of the Dred Scott decision slavery could be excluded from the territories by local legislation, became known as the Freeport Doctrine.[10]

The Collected Works gives evidence of another important aspect of Lincoln's preparation. When he was considering how to express a thought, he apparently wrote out what Basler calls "Fragment: Notes for Speeches." But instead of inserting a scrap into a speech *in toto*, Lincoln paraphrased it in context so completely that it is difficult to recognize. It is only through the editor's placement of the fragments in chronological sequence that one can tell in which speech a given passage was likely used.[11]

Newspaper reports suggest that throughout the fall Lincoln continued to repeat, rephrase, adapt, and supplement his previous speeches. He met new thrusts from Douglas, but he never budged from the stand he had taken in the House Divided speech.

An excellent sign that Lincoln had future political intentions was his interest in preserving in permanent form the newspaper reports of his important speeches, particularly his debates with Douglas. On November 19, 1858, he wrote a friend: "I hope and believe seed has been sown that will yet produce fruit. The fight must go on." After

9. Herndon and Weik, *Life of Lincoln,* 336.
10. Horace White to William Herndon, May 17, 1865, in Hertz (ed.), *Hidden Lincoln,* 271–72; Earl Schenck Miers (ed.), *Lincoln Day by Day: A Chronology, 1809–1865* (Washington, D.C., 1960), II; Joseph Medill, "A Reminiscence of Lincoln," in Edwin Erle Sparks (ed.), *The Lincoln-Douglas Debates of 1858* (Springfield, 1908), 203–204.
11. Basler (ed.), *Collected Works,* II, 547; III, 97, 205, 326, 334.

collecting accounts of his and Douglas' speeches and sponsoring their publication in the spring of 1860, he was gratified that fifty thousand copies soon sold.[12]

THE COOPER UNION ADDRESS

In his political speaking in 1859 in Ohio, Wisconsin, and Kansas, Lincoln extended his debate with Douglas, but shifted his emphasis slightly to meet three additional developments: first, because of the national interest in him, he spoke to listeners who were not yet familiar with him as a campaigner; second, Douglas, touted as a Democratic presidential candidate and one year nearer the nomination, offered a more prominent target than he had previously; third, in September, 1859, *Harper's Magazine* published a long article by Douglas that bolstered his arguments for popular sovereignty.

When invited to follow Douglas in Ohio, Lincoln prepared two more or less complete manuscripts for Columbus and Cincinnati. Since February, he had worked on a reply to Douglas and had inserted into the Columbus speech material that he had planned, but had not used, for the Kansas State Republican Convention in May. He proofread the copy of the Columbus speech and later corrected the newspaper version of the Cincinnati address. That he regarded these utterances as important is shown by his inclusion of both as campaign documents in the published volume of the Lincoln-Douglas debates. When he went to Kansas in December, 1859, he was in the midst of preparing for his Cooper Union appearance; consequently, he rehearsed some of his latest statements before Kansas listeners. His inductive development becomes evident in the progression of speeches from October, 1854, through December, 1859, with Lincoln concentrating on one issue and each speech becoming an extension of the previous one.[13]

In any study of Lincoln's speech preparation, the Cooper Union address deserves special attention, for it represents his most carefully prepared political speech and his *tour de force* against Douglas. "No

12. *Ibid.*, III, 340–43, 510; *Illinois Political Campaign of 1858: A Facsimile of the Printer's Copy of His Debates with Stephen Arnold Douglas As Edited and Prepared for Press by Abraham Lincoln* (Washington, D.C., 1958); Gerald McMurtry, "The Different Editions of the 'Debates of Lincoln and Douglas,'" *Journal of the Illinois State Historical Society*, XXVII (April, 1934), 95–107.

13. Basler (ed.), *Collected Works*, III, 400, 425ff.; Fred Brinkerhoff, "Kansas Tour of Lincoln the Candidate," *Kansas Historical Quarterly*, XIII (1934), 294–307.

former effort," reported Herndon, "had cost Lincoln so much time and thought as his Cooper Union." Realizing that the occasion required much more than the stump oratory common in rustic Illinois, Lincoln brought together the results of six years of study and testing. The proposition of his Peoria speech of October 16, 1854— "Let us return it [slavery in the territories] to the position our fathers gave it"—was the thesis of his New York address. During the 175 times that he had hammered away on that statement, he had, in his own words, "bounded it north and bounded it south and bounded it east and bounded it west."[14]

On October 12 he was invited to come to New York, and by November 1 he had agreed to speak. It is reasonable to conclude that in the three months between his acceptance of the invitation and the speech, Lincoln, with Herndon's aid, searched for proof to substitute for the circumstantial evidence he had relied on previously. He worked through materials in the state library and pored over Jonathan Elliot's *Debates in the Several State Conventions on the Adoption of the Federal Constitution* (a copy of which he owned), the *Congressional Globe*, and the *Annals of Congress*. He consulted old newspaper files and the clippings that he and Herndon had collected. How much he discussed his analysis with Herndon and the young men studying in his office is not known. Henry B. Rankin gave us a view of Lincoln at work. "He never considered anything he had written to be finished until published, or if a speech, until he delivered it. . . . It was past the middle of February before the speech was completed in its first form and put into the folder ready for Lincoln's departure. But even later, every day until it was placed in the traveling satchel, he took out the sheets and carefully went over the pages, making notations here and there, and even writing whole pages over again."[15]

The process of revision continued after Lincoln reached New York. When invited out to dinner on Sunday, February 26, Lincoln excused himself, saying: "I have not fully prepared the speech that I am to deliver Monday night. I must go over to the Astor House and work on it." When he appeared on the platform, he had a well-conceived and

14. Herndon and Weik, *Life of Lincoln*, 368; John P. Gulliver, "A Talk with Abraham Lincoln," *Independent*, XVI (December 1, 1864), 1.
15. James A. Briggs to Abraham Lincoln, telegram, October 12, 1859, in David C. Mearns, *Lincoln Papers* (2 vols.; Garden City, N.Y., 1948), I, 227, 229; Charles C. Nott to Lincoln, February 9, 1860, in Mearns, *Lincoln Papers*, 229; Herndon and Weik, *Life of Lincoln*, 368; Henry B. Rankin, *Lincoln's Cooper Institute Speech* (Springfield, Ill., 1917), 3.

revised manuscript from which he spoke; whether he read it or merely held it in his hand was unclear. Apparently the audience was impressed by his oratorical power. After delivering the speech, Lincoln probably stopped at the office of the New York *Tribune* to proofread what was to appear the following morning in four New York papers and later in the *Illinois State Journal* and the Chicago *Press and Tribune*. The speech was circulated in pamphlet form as well.[16]

THE FAREWELL ADDRESS, SPRINGFIELD

It may seem that Lincoln's beautiful farewell address, supposedly an impromptu delivery at the railroad station just before his departure for Washington, has little to tell about his speech preparation. However, the few sentences of this address help to reveal how his mind worked. Before speaking, Lincoln had apparently formulated what he wanted to say. He showed how clearly he had conceived these lines when he repeated them on the train in answer to a request; his reconstruction was almost identical to what a reporter had taken down in shorthand.[17]

THE FIRST INAUGURAL ADDRESS

The evolution of the First Inaugural Address provides one of the best examples of Lincoln at work on an important speech and gives detailed insight into his editing of three versions of this famous document. This longest of his presidential speeches, prepared in the midst of crisis, was the result of long, painful pondering, meticulous composition, and thorough review. Every word, phrase, and sentence was tested and retested for possible political implication and public reaction. Lincoln started his preparation soon after the election in November, 1860. As a first step, on November 13 he borrowed from the state library Volumes I and II of *The Statesman's Manual: Presidential Messages*, an anthology that included past inaugural addresses. Perhaps seeking a model for his own speech, Lincoln had time to peruse the volumes at some length, for he did not return them to the library until December 29.[18]

Once the election was over, the president-elect became the center of interest, with many people demanding his time. He moved from his

16. Henry B. Rankin, *Intimate Character Sketches of Abraham Lincoln* (Philadelphia, 1924), 182–83.

17. Henry Villard, *Memoirs* (2 vols.; Boston, 1904), I, 149.

18. Amy Louise Sutton, "Lincoln and Son Borrow Books," *Illinois Libraries*, XLVIII (June, 1966), 443–44.

law office to more commodious quarters in the capitol and later to the Johnson Building, an office building in Springfield. An endless stream of reporters, artists, advisers, old friends, and office seekers made serious concentration impossible; consequently, Lincoln attempted to limit his office hours and to hide away for reflection in one of three retreats. One was the editor's room at the *Illinois State Journal*. The second was a room at the St. Nicholas Hotel, an improvised studio where sculptor Thomas D. Jones worked on a bust of Lincoln. Each morning Lincoln went there for one hour to sit for the artist and to work on his correspondence and speeches. Jones reported: "Not long after taking my first sitting of Lincoln, he commenced preparing his addresses to be delivered in the different cities through which he was to pass from Springfield to Washington. His speeches or addresses were very deliberately composed, in my room. I sharpened all the Fabers he required. He generally wrote with a small portfolio and paper resting on his knee, with a copy of his published speeches lying beside him for reference. After completing one of his compositions he would very modestly read it to me."[19]

It was in a third hideaway that Lincoln did most of his work on the First Inaugural Address. During his final weeks in Springfield, when he could find "no privacy by day or night," his brother-in-law, Clark M. Smith, "fitted up a room in the third story over his store for Lincoln's use." It "could be entered only through the private office of Mr. Smith in the back part of his large storeroom," and only a limited few knew of the arrangement. Lincoln could be seen only "by persons bringing a line to Mr. Smith by Herndon."[20]

Henry Rankin wrote of carrying materials to Lincoln at this place.

I was sent twice by Herndon with books and clippings which the latter, at Lincoln's request, had selected from the State Library, the law office, and Herndon's home library, for study before preparing that remarkable state paper. On my return the last time, Herndon asked me if any word was sent back. I replied that I had no message and was sure Lincoln had not seen me when I came in and placed the packages on the table before him, or when I left the room. To this he replied with a satisfied smile, "That's what I expected; he wishes nothing now so much as to be left alone."[21]

It is through Herndon that we know what materials Lincoln

19. Thomas D. Jones, "A Sculptor's Recollections of Lincoln," in Wilson (ed.), *Lincoln Among His Friends*, 259.
20. Rankin, *Intimate Sketches*, 146–47.
21. *Ibid.*, 147–48.

consulted in his preparation. Herndon said that "sometime in January or February 1861" Lincoln asked him to help locate "Henry Clay's great, his best speech in 1850" and "likewise told me to get him President Jackson's Proclamation against Nullification in 1832–33, I think, and the Constitution." He reported that Lincoln "was perfectly familiar" with Webster's debates with both Robert Y. Hayne in 1829 and John C. Calhoun in 1833 and that Lincoln thought Webster's reply to Hayne "was the very best speech that was ever delivered."[22]

Whether these sources were all the things that Lincoln consulted, no one knows. Since he worked alone and was very secretive about what he intended to say, Herndon did not observe him at work. Further, Herndon made his recollections twenty-five years later. At no place does the younger man suggest that he helped or conferred with Lincoln. In fact, only David Davis, Francis P. Blair, Carl Schurz, Simeon Francis, Orville H. Browning, and William Seward knew what Lincoln intended to say until the day of the inauguration. Once he had completed his first draft (referred to as the First Edition), probably sometime in late January, Lincoln had it printed in eight numbered pages at the office of the *Illinois State Journal*. After further revision he had a Second Edition printed. He continued to work on this draft, which he took to Washington.[23]

During the time between his election and his taking office, Lincoln remained noncommittal about the developing national problems; he was careful not to divulge how he intended to meet the crisis or what he intended to say on March 4. When his friend George D. Prentice, editor of the Louisville *Journal*, on February 2 asked for an advance copy of the inaugural speech, Lincoln replied, "I have the document already blocked out, but in the now rapidly shifting scene, I shall have to hold it subject to revision up to near the time of delivery." He continued this reluctance on the twelve-day trip to Washington. Undoubtedly, each time he reread what he had planned, he again weighed each word and phrase, considering possible interpretations and reactions, hoping not to intensify the crisis.[24]

It is possible to follow the changes that Lincoln made and the suggestions of his two confidants, Orville H. Browning and William

22. Hertz (ed.), *Hidden Lincoln*, 118.
23. Basler (ed.), *Collected Works*, IV, 249n; Kenneth Stampp, *And the War Came* (Baton Rouge, La., 1950), 198.
24. Basler (ed.), *Collected Works*, IV, 184, 202, 249–71.

Seward, because five copies of the Second Edition, containing editorial changes, are extant. Roy P. Basler included in *The Collected Works* revealing footnotes showing alterations of the Second and Final Editions.

En route to Washington, in Indianapolis on February 11, Lincoln asked Browning to read the speech, but to show it to no one except his wife. Browning returned his copy on February 17 with only one suggestion, which Lincoln accepted.[25]

Shortly after arriving in Washington, Lincoln requested that his future secretary of state, William Seward, review the manuscript. Numbering the lines, Seward worked through the draft and made six pages of suggestions, most of which involved no more than an "inverted comma," a word, or a phrase. However, he proposed the deletion of two early paragraphs (a change that Lincoln accepted) and a complete recasting of the conclusion. On February 24, Seward returned the manuscript and explained in a cover letter, "I have suggested many changes, of little importance severally, but their general effect, tending to soothe the public mind."[26] Lincoln asked his secretary, John Nicolay, to transfer Seward's suggestions to a fresh copy, from which Lincoln worked. Since the Seward work copy is extant, it is possible to ascertain Seward's influence on the final address. He proposed forty-nine alterations, including substantial changes in three paragraphs, and Lincoln incorporated twenty-seven of these in his final address, sometimes changing a word, adding a phrase, or rewriting a sentence. Lincoln made minor changes, as illustrated by the following:

LINCOLN	SEWARD
"on the whole"	"generally"
"A disruption . . . is menaced, and"	"A disruption . . . heretofore"
"so far as can be"	"only menace is"
"on paper is already effected"	"formidably attempted"
"legally nothing"	"void"

25. Orville H. Browning's copy of First Inaugural Address (MS in Henry E. Huntington Library, San Marino, Calif.; photostatic copies of Second and Final Editions have been deposited in Illinois State Historical Library, Springfield); Maurice Baxter, *Orville H. Browning: Lincoln's Friend and Critic* (Bloomington, Ind., 1957), 109.
26. Frederic Bancroft, *The Life of William H. Seward* (2 vols.; New York, 1900), II, 24–25.

"tangible way"	"authoritative manner"
"will have its own and defended itself"	"Constitutionally defends and maintains itself"
"is against"	"imperfectly supports"

In the following phrases, the bracketed material represents insertions recommended by Seward: "Cheerly given [in every case and all circumstances] to all state"; "that [in the view of the constitution and the laws] the Union; "I shall take care [as the constitution itself expressed enjoins upon me] that the law; "as well enforced [perhaps] as any law."27

In a brief discussion it is difficult to summarize the net effect of Lincoln's total revision of the First Inaugural Address. He deleted or inserted numerous words and phrases. In at least eight cases he rewrote sentences. In one instance, at Seward's suggestion he reduced 150 words to 33; in another, 42 to 13. He expanded some sections and recast the conclusion. His main goals were to eliminate threatening and ambiguous language and to assert forcefully that his proposals were sanctioned by the Constitution. The following passages illustrate this attempt to establish legitimacy (with phrases that Lincoln incorporated into the final text indicated in brackets).

I therefore consider that [in view of the Constitution and the laws] the Union is unbroken; and, to the extent of my ability, I shall take care, [as the Constitution itself expressly enjoins upon me] that the laws of the Union be faithfully executed in all the States.

A majority [held in restraint by constitutional checks, and limitations, and always changing easily, with deliberate changes of popular opinions and sentiments] is the only true sovereign of a free people.28

Seward exercised his greatest influence upon Lincoln's famous conclusion. Following are Seward's suggestions and Lincoln's polished sentences, respectively.

I close. We are not we must not be aliens or enemies but fellow countrymen and brethren. Although passion has strained our bonds of affection too hardly they must not, I am sure they will not be broken. The mystic chords which proceeding from so many battle fields and so many patriot graves pass through all the hearts and all the hearths in this broad continent of ours will yet again harmonize in their ancient music when breathed upon by the guardian angel of the nation.

27. Basler (ed.), *Collected Works*, IV, 249–71 (footnotes).
28. *Ibid.*, IV, 265, 268.

I am loth to close. We are not enemies, but friends. We must not be enemies. Though passion may have strained, it must not break our bonds of affection. The mystic chords of memory, stretching from every battle-field, and patriot grave, to every living heart and hearthstone, all over this broad land, will yet swell the chorus of the Union, when again touched, as surely they will be, by the better angels of our nature.[29]

It is evident that Lincoln was guided considerably by Seward's suggestions, but Lincoln made them more graceful and poetic. Some of Seward's language came through, but in a style that was definitely Lincoln's own. Seward probably had more influence on strategy than ideology. Basler suggests that this address showed "the artist deliberately at work, bringing his own peculiar pattern of thought and rhythm to another man's ideas, substituting his own exact and concrete words for orotund and vague terms."[30]

Lincoln must have worked on the address almost up to the time of delivery. James G. Randall wrote that Lincoln carried to the platform "a patchwork of pastings, deletions, insertions, and printed residues." From that patchwork, Lincoln read; he then turned it over to the Washington *Star* to be set into type.[31]

THE GETTYSBURG ADDRESS

Comparatively little is known about how Lincoln worked on his speeches in the White House, but it is known that he continued to do his own work, never using a ghostwriter. The only exceptions were the little speeches that he read at the presentations of foreign ministers. These were probably written by Seward.[32]

As early as July 4, 1861, in a special message, Lincoln hinted at the theme he was to elaborate on in the Gettysburg Address: "And this issue embraces more than the fate of these United States. It presents to the whole family of man, the question, whether a constitutional republic, or a democracy—a government of the people, by the same people—can or cannot maintain its territorial integrity against its own domestic foes."[33]

---

29. *Ibid.*, IV, 261–62n99, 271.
30. Roy P. Basler, "Abraham Lincoln's Rhetoric," *American Literature*, XI (May, 1939), 181.
31. James G. Randall, *Lincoln, the President* (4 vols.; New York, 1945–55), I, 301.
32. Francis B. Carpenter, *Six Months with Lincoln in the White House* (New York, 1866), 128–29.
33. Basler (ed.), *Collected Works*, IV, 426.

Lincoln may have commenced to think about the address he was to give at Gettysburg when on November 2, 1863, he was invited to deliver "a few appropriate remarks." Although he had two weeks to prepare, it is doubtful whether he had time to consider the speech until the day before he went to Gettysburg. In those two weeks interim he "was extremely busy with important and complicated military affairs . . . [and] also with consideration of his annual message to Congress." Over thirty years later, Nicolay wrote: "There is no decisive record of when Mr. Lincoln wrote the first sentence of his proposed Address. He probably followed his usual habit in such matters, using great deliberation in arranging his thoughts and molding his phrases mentally, waiting to reduce them to writing until they had taken satisfactory form."[34]

Three recollections, however, also made long after the event, provide insights into how the eloquent sentences were developed. The first comes from a reporter and friend, Noah Brooks, one of the better sources on Lincoln's activities. Brooks related that while accompanying the president to a studio for a photographic session on Sunday, November 15, he saw in Lincoln's hand a prepublication copy of Edward Everett's address, set into type by the Boston *Journal*; critics, however, have questioned the accuracy of this date. When Brooks asked about his preparation, Lincoln reportedly said: "It is not exactly written. It is not finished, anyway. I have written it over two or three times, and I shall have to give it another lick before I am satisfied. But it is short, short, short." Ward H. Lamon remembered that a day or two before the dedication, Lincoln indicated that he had not prepared his remarks. He supposedly drew from a pocket "a sheet of fool's cap . . . closely written," which he read, remarking that it was "a memorandum of his intended address." Lamon said that what Lincoln read "proved to be in substance if not in exact words, what was afterwords printed as his famous Gettysburg Speech." A third witness, James Speed (who was later appointed attorney general), recalled that Lincoln told him that "he partially wrote it [the Gettysburg Address] before he left Washington and finished it up after arriving at Gettysburg." Much of what these three men remembered after so many years is open to question, but they agree that Lincoln wrote at least part of the address before leaving Washington. They all made recollections

34. John G. Nicolay, "Lincoln's Gettysburg Address," *Century*, XLVII (February, 1894), 596–97.

before the first draft, the original version, or the reading copy was generally available for study.[35]

The reading copy, a two-page manuscript in Lincoln's handwriting, gives evidence that its two parts were prepared at different times and probably at different places. The text of the first page, 163 words in nineteen lines, is written in ink on stationery bearing the letterhead *Executive Mansion*. Nicolay states that since the page ends with an incomplete sentence, "we may infer that at the time of writing it in Washington the remainder of the address was also written in ink on another piece of paper."[36]

The second page, a half sheet of bluish gray, diplomatic-size foolscap with wide lines, is written with a lead pencil. In the last line of the first page, Lincoln lined out the words "to stand here" and substituted "we here be dedica——" above in pencil. He then continued in pencil with the ten lines (73 words) on the second page. It is now the judgment of authorities, including Nicolay, that this second page was written at night and perhaps completed on the morning of November 19 in the upstairs room of David Will's Gettysburg home, where Lincoln had spent the night. What cannot be ascertained is whether Lincoln wrote from notes, revised a page that he had prepared before leaving Washington, or composed these famous lines of the second page after his arrival in Gettysburg. The conflicting testimony about the development of this speech explains why David C. Mearns and Lloyd A. Dunlap, who have written the best account of the occasion, concluded, "The definitive story of Lincoln and the writing of the [Gettysburg] address has not been told, nor is it likely that it ever can be."[37]

THE SECOND INAUGURAL ADDRESS

Even less than what is known about the Gettysburg Address is recorded about the evolution of the Second Inaugural Address. The terrible months of his first term had caused Lincoln to attempt to make sense out of the raging conflict. With his characteristic deliberateness,

35. Noah Brooks, "Personal Reminiscences of Lincoln," *Scribner's Monthly*, XV (February, 1878), 465; Ward H. Lamon, *Recollection of Abraham Lincoln, 1847–1865*, ed. Dorothy Lamon (Chicago, 1895), 170–71; James Speed to John E. Sutherland, New York *Times*, April 20, 1887, p. 4.

36. Facsimile of "The Nicolay Copy: the First Draft," in *Long Remembered: The Gettysburg Address in Facsimile* (Washington, D.C., 1963); Nicolay, "Lincoln's Gettysburg Address," 601.

37. David C. Mearns and Lloyd A. Dunlap, "The Preparation of the Address," in *Long Remembered*.

he devoted many solitary moments to the problem of explaining that the goal was worth the sacrifice.[38]

Two episodes suggest that he was moving toward a resolution of the dilemma. On or about April 4, 1864, Lincoln told a Kentucky delegation made up of Governor Thomas E. Bramlette, former senator Archibald Dixon, and newspaper editor Albert G. Hodges:

> If slavery is not wrong, nothing is wrong. I can not remember when I did not so think and feel. . . . I claim not to have controlled events, but confess plainly that events have controlled me. Now, at the end of three years struggle the nation's condition is not what either party or any man devised or expected. God alone can claim it. Whether it is tending seems planned. If God now wills the removal of a great wrong, and wills also that we of the North as well as you of the South, shall pay fairly for our complicity in that wrong, impartial history will find therein new cause to attest and revere the justice and goodness of God.[39]

This passage anticipated the central idea of his Second Inaugural Address. "Neither party expected for the war, the magnitude or the duration which it has already attained."[40]

In December, 1864, Lincoln was confronted by the wives of two Confederate prisoners. In arguing for mercy, one told the president that her husband was a religious man. In his reply Lincoln expressed a theme that he later incorporated into the inaugural address. "You say your husband is a religious man; tell him when you meet him, that I say I am not much of a judge of religion, but that, in my opinion, the religion that sets men to rebel and fight against their government because as they think, that government does not sufficiently help *some* men to eat their bread on the sweat of other men's faces is not the sort of religion upon which people can get to heaven."[41]

It is significant that on these two occasions Lincoln took pains after the interviews to write out what he had said impromptu. Did he realize that under pressure he had expressed a sentiment for which he had been groping? Louis A. Warren, who made the study of Lincoln his life's work, writes that this second passage found its source in the third chapter of *Genesis*: "In the sweat of thy face shall thou eat bread." He also pointed out that in the twenty-five sentences of the Second

38. Louis A. Warren, "Sources of the Second Inaugural Address," *Lincoln Lore*, No. 1352 (March 7, 1955).

39. Basler (ed.), *Collected Works*, VII, 281–83.

40. *Ibid.*, VIII, 332–33.

41. *Ibid.*, VIII, 154–55.

Inaugural Address, Lincoln mentioned the Deity fourteen times and prayer three times and in addition "paraphrased or used verbatim four biblical quotations." It is little wonder, then, that the Second Inaugural Address has sometimes been called Lincoln's Sermon on the Mount.[42]

Francis B. Carpenter, an artist who lived in the White House six months, gives us the sole picture of Lincoln engaged in the preparation of the address. "I was sitting in the President's office . . . the Sunday evening before the reinauguration, when Mr. Lincoln came in through the side passage which had lately been constructed, holding in his hand a roll of manuscripts. 'Lots of wisdom in that document, I suspect,' said he; 'it is what will be called my "second inaugural," containing about six hundred words. I will put it away here in this drawer until I want it.'"[43]

The shortness of the address, the echoing of what he had said in the two interviews, and the incorporation of familiar biblical allusions and language suggest that Lincoln had perhaps formulated the speech in his mind much the way he did his farewell address in Springfield in February, 1861. Once he had determined and arranged his ideas mentally, he may not have needed much time for the actual writing.

Views of Lincoln preparing for campaigns and important speeches provide some insights into his rhetorical persona. Close observers agreed that in analyzing a case, making a decision, writing an editorial or a letter, or preparing a speech, Lincoln was "slow, calculating, methodical and accurate" as well as logical. Referring to the development of the Gettysburg Address, Nicolay emphasized that the president "followed his usual habit in such matters using great deliberation in arranging his thoughts and molding his phrases mentally, waiting to reduce them to writing until they had taken satisfactory form." Henry B. Rankin, who was a law student in the Lincoln-Herndon office from 1856 to 1860, speaks of Lincoln's "power to concentrate strictly all his mental faculties on the task or purpose immediately before him. In this mood he was absolutely impenetrable to anything else, or by any other person. He was thoroughly oblivious

---

42. Brooks, "Personal Reminiscences," 566; Warren, "Sources of the Second Inaugural"; Louis A. Warren, "Biblical Influences in the Second Inaugural Address," *Lincoln Lore*, No. 1226 (October 6, 1952).

43. Carpenter, *Six Months with Lincoln*, 234.

to surroundings." These observations may help answer the question of whether Lincoln read his speeches or merely held the manuscript in his hand while speaking. With his power of concentration and excellent recall, he was able to deliver what he had meticulously put on paper, permitting him to speak without referring to his manuscript.[44]

None of the recollections about Lincoln suggest that he turned to others for help in formulating strategy and ideas. He stood alone, doing his own thinking and research, working in his own way, and depending little upon his associates for help. Friends and colleagues became sounding boards but little more. Because of his years of association with Lincoln, Herndon may have assisted his partner at times, particularly in 1858, and they must have discussed political developments at length. Herndon was most modest in his claims about influencing Lincoln's thinking or selection of materials, his role being mainly that of the errand boy sent to locate needed books.

Once a speech was in manuscript, Lincoln sometimes asked his friends to listen to what he had written, as with the House Divided speech and his questions for Stephen Douglas at the Freeport debate. In such cases Lincoln did not let his confidants change what he had conceived. Only in the case of the First Inaugural Address did Lincoln turn to others for critical readings and specific advice about strategy and phraseology. And in that lone instance he accepted many of Browning's and Seward's changes but remained master of his own rhetoric, transforming their suggestions into his own language with its characteristic rhythms.

44. Whitney, *Life on the Circuit*, 120; Rankin, *Intimate Sketches*, 145–46.

V

THE FIRST INAUGURAL ADDRESS
A Study of Strategy and Persuasion

James G. Randall, a preeminent Lincoln authority, aptly describes Abraham Lincoln's First Inaugural Address as "compass and chart—standards, reasonings, declarations of faith, assurances, persuasions . . . a focus in a fateful and shifting story." Informed readers place it among the great American documents, ranking it highly for its wisdom and its literary quality. But critics sometimes show awareness of little more than what appears on the printed page, neglecting its context and saying almost nothing about its immediate rhetorical goals, composition, and delivery. These critics fail to take into account that it was above all a persuasive speech, strategically directed toward specific groups of citizens and delicately tuned to lessen the imminent threat to the nation. To look only at internal characteristics, to divorce it from the tension and strife of its moment, or to fail to consider the thoughtful strivings of its creator is to misunderstand many of its immediate implications and what Lincoln determined was expedient to say to his troubled countrymen. To place the address in context, however, the interpreter should heed the advice of historian David M. Potter. "To understand Lincoln's plans at the time of his inauguration, therefore, it is necessary to exclude the misleading perspective of hindsight, and to view the problem as he viewed it at the time, rather than as he later viewed it—to distinguish sharply between his intensions [sic] for dealing with it, and his later action in dealing with it. This in turn, requires a close scrutiny of every indication as to Lincoln's attitude at a time when he refused to publicize his views."[1]

What immediate problems did Lincoln encounter on March 4, 1861? In his own words, he faced a "great and peculiar difficulty . . . a

---

1. James G. Randall, "Lincoln's Great Declaration of Faith," *New York Times Magazine*, February 6, 1949, Sec. 6, p. 11; David M. Potter, *Lincoln and His Party in the Secession Crisis* (New Haven, 1942), 315–16.

disruption of the Federal Union." As a seasoned speaker, the president-elect had concluded after long deliberation that the customary epideictic oratory would not satisfy public anxiety. He knew that the time had come for a policy statement, explicit but subtle. This chapter is developed in two parts. The first discusses the strategy of Lincoln in meeting his immediate problems. The second considers the basic ideas or standards that would guide his administration whether it faced peaceful reconciliation or war.

During the four months after the election, men and events had conspired to make the day of the inaugural dramatic and awesome. Lincoln had added to the turmoil by "a Sphinx like silence," making no speeches, issuing no public statements, and severely restricting what his representatives said in his behalf.[2] When asked to clarify his position, he had replied that he deemed it his duty to "wait until the last moment for a development of the present national difficulty" before he expressed "decidedly what course" he should pursue. En route to Washington on February 19, he told New Yorkers that he had avoided public speaking in order to give full consideration to the proper course for him to take.[3]

Why had Lincoln turned reticent? Probable explanations include his realization that he was in no position to check dissension and hysteria, for he had little power beyond the force of his mere words; contrary counsel from his advisers; a lack of solidification of northern opinion; and the impotence of the outgoing Buchanan administration in meeting the strategies of southern fire-eaters. In addition, Lincoln faced a flurry of alarming rumors, from the refusal of the House of Representatives to certify his election to aggression by the Confederacy. Furthermore, he had concluded that ill-chosen words or unwise signals about policy might result in irreparable damage before he had the power to act.

On his twelve-day trip to Washington, Lincoln had certainly heightened the tension by his behavior, which, according to Potter, was "evasive, trite and often flippant" (perhaps a little too harsh a judgment). To reporters and to many of his own party, his kind references to southerners and his apparent lack of concern about secession made no sense. For example, at Cincinnati on February 12,

2. Charles Francis Adams, *An Autobiography* (Boston, 1916), 75–77.
3. Roy P. Basler (ed.), *The Collected Works of Abraham Lincoln* (9 vols.; New Brunswick, N.J., 1953), IV, 202, 230.

and at other stops, he had "extended . . . a cordial good will to those in the far South." At a time when the walls seemed to be crumbling, Lincoln suggested in Pittsburgh that all parties should "keep cool." Is it surprising that one person called him "a simple Susan" and another ridiculed him for "perambulating the country, kissing little girls and growing whiskers"?[4] Critics did not know where he stood and wondered if he had "grossly underestimated" and "totally misconceived" the nature of the crisis, the southern temper, and secession.[5]

In spite of the consternation all around him, Lincoln had continued to maintain the appearance of being undisturbed and almost unaware of the crisis. But contrary to what some historians have suggested, Lincoln's correspondence indicates that he had received private intelligence about developments in Washington from Thomas Corwin, Salmon P. Chase, William H. Seward, Leonard Swett, Lyman Trumbull, and E. B. Washburne.[6]

It is entirely possible that the shrewd Lincoln had engaged in an act and that behind feigned appearances and impressions he had a well-conceived plan. He had felt the need to play for time in order to get his administration in place and strengthen his leadership of a young party, untested under crisis conditions. Prior to taking over the government, Lincoln had not wanted to limit his maneuverability.

No inaugural address in American history had ever been delivered under the conditions of tremendous anxiety that faced Lincoln, surrounded by gloom, uncertainty, and hatred. General Winfield Scott had put Washington under an armed alert. The bars and streets were filled with wild rumors—plots to thwart the inauguration, attempts to seize the city, threats on Lincoln's life, and secession of additional states. Hundreds of unhappy southerners were caught without the means of returning home. The only two Federal forts not in Confederate hands were under siege. The army and the government offices were demoralized by uncertain loyalties.[7]

One way to gain insight into Lincoln's strategy as expressed in the First Inaugural Address is to scrutinize the advice that he received from two close, influential confidants, Seward and Orville H. Brown-

---

4. Potter, *Lincoln and His Party*, 317; George S. Merriam, *Life and Times of Samuel Bowles* (New York, 1885), 318; Adams, *Autobiography*, 82.

5. Potter, *Lincoln and His Party*, 316.

6. David C. Mearns, *Lincoln Papers* (2 vols.; Garden City, N.Y., 1948), II, 363–65, 371–73, 376–79, 382–84, 400–402, 406–407, 421–25, 427–29, 434–35.

7. Potter, *Lincoln and His Party*, 315–33.

ing. Seward's counsel was contained in the cover letter that he wrote on February 24, 1861, to explain five pages of revisions that he had suggested after reading a proposed draft. Familiar with the Washington scene, this adept political operator thought that Lincoln should "soothe the public mind" and was most concerned about the risk of giving advantage to "the disunionists" who might attempt to force Maryland and Virginia to secede. He calculated that a wrong move might mean that "within ninety, perhaps within sixty days" the government would be "obligated to fight the South for the capital with a divided North at its back and without "one loyal magistrate or ministerial officer south of the Potomac." Aware of how such a blow would reflect on the Republican party, Seward warned, "In that case the dismemberment of the Republic would date from the inauguration of a Republican administration."[8]

Lincoln paid thoughtful attention to what his future secretary of state said, for he respected Seward as astute and well informed about the temper of leaders from both the North and the South. Seward's letter left little doubt that he and Lincoln agreed on the necessity of playing for time and of directing their efforts toward the citizens of the upper South. How well the two men understood each other about the policy beyond the following six to eight weeks is not known. Seward hoped, according to Charles Francis Adams, "to divide the South by conciliating the northern tier of Slave States, including Virginia especially; and holding them loyal until the tide of reaction, setting in, should drive the seceding states into a false position from which they would ultimately be compelled to recede. . . . He had formulated a policy based on the careful avoidance of a collision and bloodshed until there had been ample time allowed for reflection and the saving second thought."[9]

Among the uncertainties facing Seward, who regarded himself as the most qualified person to make decisions for the new administration, were Lincoln's stand on other vital issues and the kind of role Lincoln would play in decision making. Although little is known of Lincoln's thoughts, his view on reconciliation was probably similar to Seward's. At this time few persons, including the president-elect, had squarely faced the issue of civil war.

8. John G. Nicolay and John Hay, *Abraham Lincoln: A History* (10 vols.; New York, 1904), III, 319–20.
9. Adams, *Autobiography*, 73.

The second person Lincoln asked to read his inaugural address was Orville Browning, a conservative, long-time friend and fellow lawyer. On the trip to Washington, Lincoln had presented to Browning what he called "the First Edition" and had asked for advice. Browning found only one paragraph that he thought needed changing. In a paragraph on recovering Federal property seized by the Confederate states, Lincoln had written, "All power at my disposal will be used to reclaim the public property," a position that he had reiterated several times in the previous three months and that was popular with radical Republicans. Browning advised Lincoln to follow a course of moderation and recommended a softening of the language. Although he agreed that "fallen places ought to be reclaimed," he asked, "Cannot that be accomplished as well or even better without announcing the purpose in the inaugural?" Lincoln found the suggestion consistent with his tendency toward understatement. Like Seward, Browning warned against inflammatory language that seemed threatening, "particularly to the border states." This strategy was designed to thwart the secessionists who were looking for a justification to make the break decisive and thereby pull the border states over to their side.[10]

On March 4, 1861, when Lincoln looked over the vast gathering awaiting his inaugural address in the open air, what a contrast the simple, six-foot-four Illinois lawyer offered to many of his adversaries: fiery southerners such as Louis T. Wigfall of Texas, Robert Toombs of Georgia, and William L. Yancey of Alabama; northern radicals such as Charles Sumner of Massachusetts; and recent opponents John C. Breckinridge, Stephen Douglas, and John Bell. When he stepped forward on "the miserable scaffold," a temporary platform on the east side of the Capitol, laid aside his cane, passed his new hat to Douglas (a guest on the platform), took his steel-framed spectacles from a pocket, and read from his manuscript, Lincoln projected little of the popular contemporary view of the orator or the confident statesman. Many who saw and heard him that day pondered whether this simple, angular man was equal to the problems ahead. They could not know how shrewd, persistent, and calculating he would be over the next four years.[11]

---

10. Theodore Calvin Pease and James G. Randall (eds.), *Diary of Orville Hickman Browning* (2 vols.; Springfield, Ill., 1925), I, 455–56; Maurice Baxter, *Orville H. Browning: Lincoln's Friend and Critic* (Bloomington, Ind., 1957), 108–10.

11. Charles Aldrich, "At Lincoln's First Inauguration," *Annals of Iowa*, 3rd Ser., VIII (April,

The president-elect had to deal with negative portrayals of his public image. His political opponents had attacked him as an abolitionist and a supporter of John Brown. An unfriendly press, in both the North and the South, had viciously maligned him and his wife. Aristocratic southerners had dismissed him as an ignorant poor white and pointed to his election as the reason for secession. Even members of his own party wavered in their enthusiasm for him as a leader. What Lincoln needed most was to remove this stigma and build confidence in his ability to lead, doing nothing to discredit his administration and at the same time asserting his trustworthiness. He stated that the inaugural must be his "certificate of moral character."[12]

Significantly, his strategy in adjusting to the current crisis was to cast his remarks in a nonpersonal vein, speaking for the most part from the third-person point of view, qualifying his answers, remaining somewhat abstract, and saying almost nothing about the programs of his forthcoming administration. Lincoln divorced himself from the conflict and avoided expressions of partisanship. In a first draft he had written "on our side and yours," but in his final draft he altered the sentence to read "on your side of the North or yours of the South." He used the first person in identifying his own opinions and activities, but he seemed to prefer the persona of simply a Republican administration, the national authority, or the president, the servant of the majority, restricted by the Constitution, the law, and his oath. He once referred to "all the published speeches of him who addresses you," thereby shifting the focus to the office and its required duties, not himself and his personal preferences. He generally avoided a familiar point of view in speaking of the two parties involved and resorted to references to groups: all members of Congress, the state, the majority, the minority, the Union, one section or another, the country. In only one sentence did he refer to North or South, and he made no mention of the Confederacy, secessionists, party affiliation, or enemies.[13] Throughout his speaking he sought to strengthen his credibility and to appear judicious, thoughtful, and law-abiding. He read his manuscript without flourish, holding closely to what he had meticulously

---

1907), 47; Kenneth M. Stampp, *And The War Came: The North and the Secession Crisis, 1860–1861* (Baton Rouge, 1950), 197–203.

12. Ward H. Lamon, *Recollections of Abraham Lincoln, 1847–1865* (Chicago, 1895), 30.

13. All quotations from the First Inaugural Address are taken from the Final Text, in Basler (ed.), *Collected Works*, IV, 262–71.

composed. One friendly reporter wrote that "its firm and explicit statements" were at the "level of the popular mind,—the plain homespun language of a man accustomed to talk with 'the folks' and 'the neighbor,' the language of a man of vital common sense, whose words exactly fit his facts and thoughts."[14]

A striking characteristic of the First Inaugural Address is that Lincoln seemed to direct so much of it toward southerners, toward those "who really love[d] the Union," or toward his "dissatisfied fellow-countrymen," and addressed so little to those "who seek to destroy the Union" and to his own partisan supporters. Agreeing with his advisers, he showed the most concern about the border states, where followers of Bell and Douglas outnumbered those who supported Breckinridge and where he was most likely to gain a thoughtful hearing. He probably hoped that pro-Union men of the Deep South, silenced at the moment by angry secessionists, might welcome friendly assurances of his position on slavery. Editor Henry J. Raymond of the New York *Times* affirmed that "Lincoln entered upon the duties of his office and addressed himself to the task, first of withholding the Border States from joining the Confederacy, as an indispensable preliminary to the great work of quelling the rebellion and restoring the authority of the Constitution."[15]

Lincoln expressed his theme when he asked "one and all [to] think calmly and well upon this whole subject." Once again he wanted to remind southerners of what he had advocated, to counter the misrepresentation of his character, and to stimulate traditional national loyalties and sentiments.

From his opening sentences Lincoln sought to relieve hysteria and fear and to foster trust in his administration. "The accession of a Republican administration," he said, had never constituted "any reasonable cause for . . . apprehension," and "the property, peace and security of no section" were "in any wise endangered by the now incoming administration." Lincoln made his assurances straightforward, reaffirming what he had often stated—that he had "no purpose, directly or indirectly to interfere with the institution of slavery where it exists" and that he would support the Fugitive Slave Act. He minimized what he could actually do under the Constitution in a brief

---

14. Boston (Mass.) *Transcript*, March 5, 1861.
15. Henry J. Raymond, *The Life and Public Service of Abraham Lincoln* (New York, 1865), 162.

four-year term and insisted that he sought a "peaceful solution" with no intention of "harassing the people," of "invasions," or of using "force against or among the people."

Lincoln chose language that was legalistic and impersonal, and he avoided highly loaded emotional terms bandied about by the press, radical Republicans, and southern agitators. Sensitive to southern attitudes, he substituted in his final draft the less harsh words *acquiesce* for *submit* and *revolutionary* for *treasonable*, and he did not dwell on the terms *coercion, invasion, recapture, submission*, or *enforcement*. In referring to the conflict, he again sought neutral phrases: some difference of opinion, disruption of the Federal Union, destruction of our national fabric, our present differences. Only once, near the end of the address, did Lincoln allude to "the momentous issue of civil war." Furthermore, he did not emotionalize what he considered an important issue, the extension of the institution of slavery in the territories. Running through Lincoln's persuasion was a strategy of reducing an issue, a threat, a problem, or a disagreement to its simplest form, thereby stripping away from the core any inflammatory overtones that complicated resolution. Lincoln argued that the new administration did not constitute a threat, that no hasty solution was demanded, and that the conflict was not serious. He brought this argument to a climax when he said: "One section of our country believes slavery is right, and ought to be extended, while the other believes it is wrong, and ought not to be extended. This is the only substantial dispute."

As a part of his strategy, Lincoln sought to establish common ground with southern countrymen through the insertion of many references to mutually held beliefs and sentiments — "our national fabric, with all its benefits, its memories, and its hopes" — thus touching the loyalties of those "who really love[d] the Union." Hoping to identify with democratic tradition, he expressed his submission to and dependence on "the people themselves," calling them "my rightful master." Likewise, he cast what he said in the context of the great cornerstones of American tradition: the Declaration of Independence, the Constitution, and the Supreme Court. Lincoln brought this fervent play upon consubstantiality to a high pitch when he dramatically stated: "Physically speaking, we cannot separate. We cannot remove our respective sections from each other, nor build an impassable wall between them. A husband and wife may be divorced, and go out of the presence, and beyond the reach of each other; but the different parts of our country cannot do this. They cannot but remain face to face; and intercourse, either amicable or hostile, must continue between them. Is it possible then to make that intercourse more advantageous, or more satisfactory, *after* separation than *before?*" In this passage he especially touched a long-felt affinity arising from the interdependence of those living along the Mason-Dixon Line and in the Ohio, Tennessee, and Mississippi river basins. His argument had long bound westerners and southerners together.

The most eloquent passage of the address, and the most often quoted, which he saved for the peroration, also played upon mutual feelings of consubstantiality. Saying he was "loth to close," Lincoln again reminded his "fellow countrymen" of their closeness and their affection for one another: "We are not enemies, but friends. We must not be enemies. Though passion may have strained, it must not break our bonds of affection. The mystic chords of memory, stre[t]ching from every battle-field, and patriot grave, to every living heart and hearthstone, all over this broad land, will yet swell the chorus of the Union, when again touched, as surely they will be, by the better angels of our nature."

These poignant, poetic sentences, recast at the suggestion of Seward, contain elements of what Kenneth Burke spoke of as identification—"bonds of affection" and "mystic chords of memory," for example.[16]

Another major characteristic of Lincoln's persuasion was his repeated effort to legitimize his position and proposals, that is, to premise what he offered on constitutional grounds, the laws of the country, the universal law of history, and precedent. In revising the First Edition (as he referred to the copy set into type before he left Springfield), Lincoln repeatedly inserted phrases to highlight his authority. For example, in one important sentence he added "*in view of the Constitution and the laws*, the Union is unbroken [emphasis added]." He insisted that, in carrying out his duties, he must be true to "the most solemn oath . . . registered in heaven" and take "the official oath . . . with no mental reservations." When he spoke of enforcing the Fugitive Slave Act, he reminded his listeners that "all members of Congress swear their support to the whole Constitution." To Lincoln

16. Kenneth Burke, A *Rhetoric of Motives* (New York, 1953), 21, 46.

the lawyer, swearing in court, taking oaths, and obeying the law and the Supreme Court were precious and binding acts.

In addition to the necessity of keeping the states of the upper South from joining the Confederacy, Lincoln had to satisfy a second public demand—to make good on his promises to state his position on the crisis at hand. For three months he had remained silent, claiming that he would give his answer to the disruption of the Union in his inaugural address. He could delay no longer. Well into his speech, he therefore advanced a basic position, or what Douglas called "a line of policy." In the persona of the chief executive, Lincoln explained that he was enjoined to execute faithfully the laws in "all the States." His basic position was worded as follows:

> I hold, that in contemplation of universal law, and of the Constitution, the Union of these States is perpetual. Perpetuity is implied, if not expressed, in the fundamental law of all national governments. It is safe to assert that no government proper, ever had a provision in its organic law for its own termination. Continue to execute all the express provisions of our national Constitution, and the Union will endure forever—it being impossible to destroy it, except by some action not provided for in the instrument itself. . . .
>
> It follows from these views that no State, upon its own mere motion, can lawfully get out of the Union—that resolves and ordinances to that effect are legally void, and that acts of violence, within any State or States, against the authority of the United States, are insurrectionary or revolutionary, according to circumstances.

His word choice again showed that he attempted to make his declaration nonthreatening and acceptable to those who might disagree, as when he spoke of "resolves and ordinances," not secession. In the last sentence, he had originally planned to use the word *treasonable*, but after consideration, he changed it to the less-charged *revolutionary*.

Lincoln projected his own role as an impersonal one: "To the extent of my ability, I shall take care, as the Constitution itself expressly enjoins upon me, that the laws of the Union be faithfully executed in all the States. Doing this I deem to be only a simple duty on my part." In expressing this thought, a less-skilled rhetor might have claimed too much and insinuated his own importance, but not the shrewd constitutional lawyer who had learned well his lessons before the Illinois Supreme Court. Lincoln presented himself as an instrument obligated to carry out a simple duty. He left his listeners probably wondering, "What else could he do?"

He was equally cautious in how he spoke about the touchy subject of the power confided to him, saying that it "will be used to hold, occupy, and possess the property and places belonging to the government." Some writers have thought that herein Lincoln practiced the strategy of avoidance, because he said nothing about *recapturing*, *reclaiming*, or *seizing* the properties taken by the southern states in the previous three months. In his first version, Lincoln had actually written, "All power at my disposal will be used to reclaim the public property and places which have fallen." In his letters, he had often written "retake," giving every indication that he intended to recapture Federal properties by force. But influenced by the advice of Browning, Lincoln modified the sentence in order to avoid further irritation, letting his listeners infer what they wished. This rhetorical strategy stated his reasonable duty without excessively stressing it and thereby alienating the border state audiences.

Lincoln's constructive case, worded adroitly, was a masterly example of understatement and perhaps indirection; what he said became the basis for future dealing with seceders. Although he granted that "a disruption of the Federal Union" had been "formidably attempted," he never recognized the Confederate states as a legal body.

It has been argued that at this juncture between peace and war, Lincoln implied in his policy statement a plan of peaceful reconciliation. His strategy of understatement was not to drive the loyal southern states into the arms of the secessionists, but to invite the states of the Deep South to return to the Union when they agreed to abide by the Constitution.

The main thrust of this chapter thus far has been to discuss Lincoln's immediate objectives, which involved retaining the loyalty of the citizens of the upper South. However, as a skilled rhetor, Lincoln planted in the address a message for the other "fellow citizens": his own party members, northern Democrats and Bellites, Unionists in the seceded states, and the secessionists.

Ward H. Lamon, who observed Lincoln closely during the inaugural address, explained the complexity of Lincoln's task of appealing to this diverse audience: "To moderate the passions of his own partisans, to conciliate his opponents in the North, and divide and weaken his enemies in the South, was a task which no mere politician was likely to perform, yet one which none but the most expert of politicians and wisest of statesmen was fitted to undertake. It requires moral as well as intellectual qualities of the highest order." But to reach this wider audience, Lincoln resorted to subtlety rather than direct declaration, leaving the clarification of specific programs to the future and letting his listeners fill in what they surmised to be his meaning.[17]

From his correspondence and interviews during the previous four months, it is clear that Lincoln was politician enough to know that he must unite the diverse elements of his own party, a minority of the electorate. Following prevailing northern opinion, Lincoln continued to emphasize the middle ground between the extremes of his party; he made preservation of the Union, not the abolition of slavery, his principal objective, thus resisting both those who wanted to let the South depart in peace and the advocates of compromise who proposed making concessions on the territorial question. Fortunately, on March 4, Lincoln felt no compulsion to declare himself on the immediate crisis at Fort Sumter.

Much of what appealed to moderate Republicans was equally attractive to northern Democrats and Bellites who agreed upon the necessity of maintaining the Union under the Constitution, but who, like many Republicans, were hesitant about aggressively protecting Federal rights in the South. Lincoln no doubt wanted to avoid forcing those with strong southern ties and sympathies to make a choice of sides before the secessionists had clearly shown their hand.

Among the long-term objectives to be attained beyond six or eight weeks from the inauguration was peaceful reconciliation. In an overture to the southern Unionists, silenced at the moment in the states of the Confederacy, Lincoln implied a method of achieving this goal: since he considered the Union perpetual and unbroken, the southern states could resume normal activities when their residents elected loyal officials. He proposed "that the laws of the Union be faithfully executed in all the states" (said probably for the benefit of northern voters) and declared that he would "hold . . . the property . . . belonging to the government" (most likely he thought of the two forts in Federal hands), but he did not mention recapturing or retaking what presently was in the hands of Confederate states. Aware of public sensitivity about invasion and coercion, he avoided suggesting aggres-

17. Ward H. Lamon, *Life of Abraham Lincoln* (Boston, 1872), 467.

sive action, promising "no invasion, no using force . . . no attempt to force obnoxious strangers [officials of the government] among the people" and no attempt to deliver mail when the citizens objected. At this moment Lincoln and Seward, caught between the equally likely possibilities of peace and war, believed naïvely that by remaining dispassionate they would provide time for pro-Union sentiment (probably from old-time Whigs in the South) to exert positive pressure on the hotheads to resume normal relations with the other states and to heal the rupture without armed conflict. Those with hindsight have declared that Lincoln totally misconceived secessionist sentiment. So he did, but he had much company throughout the North.

What did Lincoln say to the seceders? Only once, and then not until the closing paragraphs, did he address the fire-eaters, calling them "my dissatisfied fellow-countrymen." Interestingly, in referring to them as countrymen, Lincoln was refusing to concede the legality of their departure. In an adroit move to shift the responsibility of war to them, he stated, "The government will not assail you. You can have no conflict without being yourselves the aggressors." His speaking, it should be noted, was intended to be considerate and without emotional intensity, stating his position without threat or censure. Nevertheless, secessionists saw in Lincoln's remarks a declaration of war and suspected that beneath the velvet glove were determination and rigor. They were correct.

Some northern readers immediately praised Lincoln's efficacious strategy, saying that "the disunionists were hopelessly cornered" and were placed "manifestly in the wrong." Samuel Bowles, editor of the Springfield *Daily Republican*, expressed it well when he said that Lincoln had "hedge[d] them [secessionists] in so that they cannot take a single step without making treasonable war upon the government."[18]

The contrasting views of Lincoln's address became most evident in the Senate on March 6, when the question of printing it arose. Senator Thomas L. Clingman of North Carolina declared that "clearly and directly" the address "must lead to war—war against the confederate or seceding states." In contrast, Lincoln's old rival Douglas pronounced the address "a much more conservative document" and "a much more pacific and conciliatory paper" than he had expected. He continued,

18. Springfield (Mass.) *Daily Republican*, March 6, 1861, quoted in Stampp, *And the War Came*, 201.

"I am clearly of the opinion that the Administration stands pledged by the Inaugural to a peaceful solution of all our difficulties."[19]

From Lincoln's point of view, Douglas' remark was more important than Clingman's, for Douglas' indicated how northern Democrats were lining up to support the new administration and maintain the Union.

Was the First Inaugural Address well conceived in terms of the goals Lincoln hoped to achieve within six to eight weeks of the inauguration? Admittedly, the address was only a single thread in a complex fabric. However, Lincoln's strategy of delay, indirection, and caution allowed him to take office, avoid precipitate action at a critical time, and move toward keeping in the Union at least four border states: Delaware, Kentucky, Maryland, and Missouri. Douglas' statement was an indication that Lincoln was likely to enlist strong support throughout the North for maintaining the Union intact. The loss of North Carolina, Tennessee, and Virginia and the outbreak of war were perhaps predetermined long before March 4, 1861.

19. *Congressional Globe*, 36th Cong., 2nd Sess., 1436–38.

VI

THE LASTING QUALITIES OF
THE GETTYSBURG ADDRESS

Through the years I have discovered that oral examinations of doctoral candidates sometimes bring out unexpected answers. The historian T. Harry Williams, hoping to start off one of my candidates with an easy question, asked, "What is your opinion of the Gettysburg Address?" Without hesitating, the student responded, "It was a failure." Somewhat surprised to hear that conclusion coming from a student majoring in public address, Williams naturally sought clarification. The candidate confidently explained, "Lincoln did not stir his audience that day." He apparently considered the effective speech to be one that produces immediately an overt response. In expressing that opinion, the candidate was not alone in his measure of a successful speech and of the Gettysburg Address.

The declaration that the Gettysburg Address was a failure has always embarrassed me, particularly when such an assertion is made before historians and literary critics who hold Lincoln's speech in awe. The immediate-effectiveness measure makes little sense to persons who have given the address a secure place in the literature in the English language and who agree with Lord Curzon that it is among the three "supreme masterpieces of English eloquence."[1]

Of course, at the outset we must concede that many of the fifteen thousand people present on November 19, 1863, expressed little reaction to what Lincoln said in less than three minutes. One listener complained that the president had "but barely commenced when he stopped." In fact, Lincoln concluded before a photographer could get his equipment into place; consequently the only picture of the event shows a forest of stovepipe hats with the president somewhere in their midst. The principal attraction that day was the distinguished Edward Everett, whom some considered the greatest living American orator. His carefully crafted address of almost two hours overshadowed Lincoln's brief statement, which many dismissed as a ceremonial

1. William E. Barton, *Lincoln at Gettysburg* (Indianapolis, 1930), 128.

addendum. Much of what is known about the whole day was re-counted later, when great interest developed in the assassinated president. But eyewitnesses who tried to remember the memorial service at Gettysburg did not agree upon the simplest details or the part Lincoln played in it. Fortunately, two reporters transcribed what Lincoln had said, and their copies were published in the following day or two.[2]

The copy printed by the Associated Press indicates applause in five places, but many suggest that these interruptions were light and perfunctory, perhaps no more than the politeness that listeners thought was due the president. The report of the *Patriot and Union* of nearby Harrisburg referred to Lincoln's 267 words as "the silly remarks of the President," and another account called them "dull and common-place." Showing even greater bias, one critic, probably a Democrat, charged that Lincoln had "foully traduced the motives of the slain." Not confident about his reception, Lincoln is quoted as saying to his friend Ward Lamon, who was marshal of the day, that the speech "won't scour" and that it was "a flat failure" and "fell upon the audience like a wet blanket." Nevertheless, some editors soon began to sense the greatness in what the president had said, calling it "admi-rable," "a perfect gem," and a "heart to the heart" speech.[3]

The day following the service, Edward Everett wrote Lincoln, "I should be glad if I could flatter myself that I came as near to the central idea of the occasion in two hours as you did in two minutes." The editor of the Philadelphia *Evening Bulletin* lauded "the President's brief speech" as "warm, earnest, unaffected, and touching." He and other editors were reacting to printed versions, not to the speech as it was delivered. But more extravagant praise appeared twenty-five or thirty years later, after memories had faded, when a mythic Lincoln had commenced to emerge, and people were belatedly trying to put themselves into his inner circle.[4]

No one today denies the eloquence of the Gettysburg Address. But what is it? A speech? An essay? Literature? Is it a prose poem or, in Carl Sandburg's words, the "great American poem"?

2. Louis A. Warren, *Lincoln's Gettysburg Declaration* (Fort Wayne, Ind., 1964), 139–41; Svend Petersen, *Gettysburg Addresses: The Story of Two Orations* (New York, 1963), 53–64.
3. Ward H. Lamon, *Recollections of Abraham Lincoln, 1847–1865* (Chicago, 1895), 171, 175; Warren, *Lincoln's Declaration*, 143–46.
4. John G. Nicolay and John Hay, *Abraham Lincoln: A History* (10 vols.; New York, 1904), VIII, 203; Barton, *Lincoln at Gettysburg*, 161–210.

The biographer William E. Barton, a respected Lincoln authority, suggests that the address did not succeed as oratory and therefore should be judged as literature. "Decidedly, Lincoln was not an orator," says another source. "He was something else—a literary artist—and he could work only with the tool of the literary artist, his pen." These opinions probably originated in the reports that Lincoln did not immediately get a roaring ovation.[5]

Such judgments must be examined in the context of the mid-nineteenth century. Admittedly, Lincoln did not produce the kind of rhetoric popular during the golden age of American oratory, when famous orators spoke in the grand style and strove to produce "oratory for oratory's sake." Conceding that Lincoln was an excellent stump speaker, T. Harry Williams writes that he "was not a Henry, a Webster, or a Bryan." How true. "His speeches always read much better than they sounded," Williams says, explaining that Lincoln "was more interested in communicating a thought to others than in decorating it with pretty phrases." But is not this very factor a significant quality of the Gettysburg Address? Its power is in its simple thought, composition, and language—and not in the magnetism of Lincoln's personality or the "mellow beauty" of his voice. When the aspects of his manner, physical appearance, and delivery were forgotten, his ideas and language continued and will continue to endure.[6]

Perhaps some of the confusion over how to classify the Gettysburg Address stems from a misunderstanding of the ceremonial speech, its intended audience, and the desired response. Some of the writers who have expressed disappointment with the reception of the Gettysburg Address as a speech seem to hold that an orator's only concern should be the reaction of the face-to-face audience. They argue that the greater the overt response, the more effective the speech. On the contrary, we know that speakers may stir varying degrees of response, ranging from the covert to the overt, from inner deep affirmations to raucous outbursts. In this sense, a ceremonial speech is a special genre, because the commemorator or eulogist, starting with the agreement and sympathy of his listeners, may seek to heighten or

---

5. Barton, *Lincoln at Gettysburg*, 113; Herbert Joseph Edwards and John Erskine Hankins, "Lincoln the Writer: The Development of His Literary Style," *University of Maine Bulletin*, 2nd ser., LXIV (1962), 81.

6. William G. Carleton, "The Celebrity Cult a Century Ago," *Georgia Review*, XIV (1960), 133–42; T. Harry Williams (ed.), *Selected Writings and Speeches of Abraham Lincoln* (Chicago, 1943), xlviii–liii.

intensify the shared feelings not only of his immediate audience but also of those far beyond, that is, readers in the future. I have sometimes amazed my students by pointing out that even in the 1980s they, too, are members of Lincoln's audience.

Seeking a wider audience, the orator wants his words to read well so they may find a place among literary pieces. But does his striving for future admirers change the speech into an essay? In working to give his appeals wider emotional impact, the creator chooses carefully his materials and his language. He may become figurative and at times approach the poetic in his style, thereby hoping to touch readers as well as listeners.

Certainly Edward Everett had in mind his greater audience when he polished his two-hour address and made a copy available to the press before he went to Gettysburg. The day following the ceremonies, his address, along with Lincoln's, was issued in a pamphlet by the Washington *Chronicle* and published in full in several newspapers. Within six months the two speeches had been printed in nine permanent editions.

Why has the Gettysburg Address continued to live? There are at least three reasons for its popularity as a speech. First, it is the statement of a martyred president about a tremendous battle and is cherished by persons on both sides of the Mason-Dixon Line. The Gettysburg National Military Park and the town itself usually attract more than 1.5 million visitors each year. The whole area is a display of memorabilia. The establishment of the final resting place gained the immediate support of all the northern states whose soldiers fell there. Soon former Confederate states joined in erecting great monuments to their own. Few will dispute Roy P. Basler, who states, "Although the Civil War was won and lost more conclusively on other fields, the metaphor and symbol, which Emerson avowed to be the ultimate of all factual history, have come to rest not on Vicksburg or Pea Ridge, not even on Appomattox, but on Gettysburg."[7]

It is not surprising that numerous volumes recount every detail of the three-day encounter, and that over twenty books, including two major studies, have been devoted to Lincoln's brief address. In addition, numerous Lincoln biographies discuss this dramatic dedication. The ever-growing Lincoln legend has nurtured an equally

7. Roy P. Basler, *Lincoln's Gettysburg Address in Translation* (Washington, D.C., 1972), 1.

powerful myth about Lincoln's immortal words. The full text appears on postcards and wall plaques, on the side wall of the Lincoln Memorial in Washington, D.C., and on the monument at Gettysburg. But "the metaphor and symbol alone," striking as they are, probably are not enough to explain the universality of appeal of the Gettysburg Address. Something more resides in the words.

A second reason for the permanence of the address is its quotability. Along with notable passages from the Bible, it has become one of the most widely known recitations in the English language and has gained the reputation as the most recognized American speech. Elton Trueblood says that it "is far better known than are the events which it was written to commemorate."[8]

A part of the magic of this address is that it is easy to memorize and to recall. Its customary language gives it what Trueblood calls "a magnificent simplicity"; the ideas and words are familiar without being commonplace. It has the clarity of the King James Version of the Bible, and its attraction lies in its repetition, antithesis, parallelism, poetical cadence, and verbal harmony. It has fascinated a number of leading actors, readers, and poets, who have recorded it for listening, particularly in the classroom.[9]

Often more than half of the students in a given college class are able to recite the speech in whole or in part. They can identify it by a word or a phrase. Many, of course, first memorized it because of the insistence of a grade school teacher. "Of the people, by the people, and for the people" has become the hallmark of Lincoln.

Brief enough to fit on a single page, texts of it appear in histories, literature anthologies, school readers, speech textbooks, brochures, and pamphlets. Readily available for study, the five holographs are reproduced in two publications of the Government Printing Office. Volumes about Lincoln, now numbering in the thousands, seldom fail to reprint one or more versions of the full text. Fascinated, critics have studied and restudied its origins, thought, structure, language, and implications.[10]

8. Elton Trueblood, *Abraham Lincoln: Theologian of American Anguish* (New York, 1973), 134.
9. Raymond Massey, *Reading Lincoln's Gettysburg Address and Lincoln's Second Inaugural Address*, n.d. and *Raymond Massey Reads the Writing and Speeches of Abraham Lincoln*, 1961; Royal Dano, *Great Moments with Mr. Lincoln*, 1964.
10. *Abraham Lincoln's Gettysburg Address: The First and Second Drafts Now in the Library of Congress* (Washington, D.C., 1965); *Long Remembered: Facsimiles of the Five Versions of the*

But quotability also does not fully explain the lasting power of Lincoln's "few appropriate remarks." Something more resides in the composition.

The paramount reason the Gettysburg Address has endured is that it is a moving pronouncement about freedom. In a few words it encompasses the central concern of those who cherish or yearn for liberty, human dignity, and democratic values. Touching upon this common theme, Lincoln told a Chicago audience in 1858 that the proposition "all men are created equal" was "the electric cord . . . that links the hearts of patriotic and liberty loving men together, that will link those patriotic hearts as long as love of freedom exists in the minds of men throughout the world."[11] And there are millions of people, in all times and places, who sense in Lincoln's words the expression of their own striving and dreams.

Throughout his long political career, Lincoln made the Declaration of Independence the capstone of his political philosophy, and he knew that by doing so he alluded to symbols that his opponents could not and would not challenge. As a good rhetor, Lincoln saw in the Declaration a binding force to unite his fellow Americans as well as others who sought freedom abroad.

In 1863, in the midst of the Civil War, he was eager to make the common ties more evident and more binding. Fully aware that the struggle had weakened historically patriotic resolve, Lincoln knew that he must dispel gloom and feelings of hopelessness and restore the belief in the Federal government expressed by "the forefathers." He had to find words that expressed more than a popular bromide and that exceeded the standard Fourth of July oratory or the polished declamation of Edward Everett. What marks Lincoln as a superior rhetor was that he captured in ten sentences what one authority has called "the comprehensive and perfect grasping of great ideas . . . in language that is condensed, crystalline, and perfectly simple." In uttering these revered sentiments he continued the tradition of Patrick Henry, Thomas Jefferson, Daniel Webster, and his mentor, Henry Clay. Furthermore, he identified with freedom lovers throughout time.[12]

Gettysburg Address in the Handwriting of Abraham Lincoln (Washington, D.C., 1963), with notes and comments by David C. Mearns and Lloyd A. Dunlap.

11. Roy P. Basler (ed.), *The Collected Works of Abraham Lincoln* (9 vols.; New Brunswick, N.J., 1953), II, 499–500.

12. Orton H. Carmichael, *Lincoln's Gettysburg Address* (New York, 1917), 98.

Within the framework of his commemoration, he hoped to stir the resolves of the Unionists to continue the struggle to save the nation, free the slaves, and prove that a nation "so conceived and so dedicated can long endure." But what he could not know, although he hoped for it, was that after the guns were silenced, the time would come when southerners, too, would find inspiration in his words.

Their dramatic origin, their quotability, and their expression of the theme of freedom have given Lincoln's "appropriate remarks" lasting quality. The three elements have produced a speech that is held dear by people in many countries. The sentences sound as powerful today as they did 120 years ago: "A new nation conceived in liberty and dedicated to the proposition that all men are created equal. . . . That this nation, under God, shall have a new birth of freedom. . . . And that government of the people, by the people, and for the people, shall not perish from the earth."

VII

"WITH CHARITY FOR ALL"
The Second Inaugural Address as Persuasion

What historians have said of the First Inaugural Address is equally true of the Second, delivered March 4, 1865. In the words of James G. Randall, the Second was also a declaration of faith, assurance, and persuasion. The First served as the prologue; the Second, as the epilogue to "a fearful and shifting story." Coming after many difficult decisions and the great anxiety of the war, this remarkable address, compact in composition and meaning, provided revealing insights into the times as well as the innermost thoughts and feelings of the Illinois lawyer who strove to understand and meet the demands of his great burden.[1] Because it was epideictic in character, profound in thought, and eloquent in language, the address has assumed a mythic quality, as has much of Lincoln's life and thought. It has deservedly gained stature as one of the best addresses in the English language.[2] The present discussion, however, is to explain not its aesthetic quality but its practical goals in its immediate context; the focus is on the address as persuasion, that is, as an attempt to move listeners. Some, because of their reverence for the speech, may feel that such a quest is almost blasphemous. Nevertheless, Lincoln had goals to accomplish, and in the role of public speaker he was a persuader. One way to gain insight into the motivation for the address is to review the events and forces that had influenced Lincoln during the previous four months.

On March 4, because of recent developments, Lincoln had reason to be reflective and encouraged. First, he had achieved reelection with a majority of 400,000 votes, receiving a total of 2,203,831 popular votes to 1,797,019 for the Democratic candidate, George McClellan (212 electoral votes to 21 for his opponent). In his annual message to

---

1. James G. Randall, "Lincoln's Great Declaration of Faith," *New York Times Magazine*, February 6, 1949, Sec. 6, p. 11.
2. Louis A. Warren, *Lincoln's Gettysburg Declaration: A New Birth of Freedom* (Fort Wayne, Ind., 1964), 171–76.

Congress on December 6, 1864, Lincoln had said, "Judging by the recent canvass and its results, the purpose of the people within the loyal states, to maintain the integrity of the Union, was never more firm, nor more nearly unanimous, than now."[3]

Second, Lincoln was in a position to tell Congress, "Our arms have steadily advanced; thus liberating the regions left in the rear, so that Missouri, Kentucky, Tennessee, and parts of other states have again produced reasonably fair crops." Furthermore, he knew that he now had two powerful, well-directed, advancing armies under Grant and William T. Sherman that were squeezing the Confederate forces into ever-smaller areas.[4]

Third, on January 31, 1865, Congress had passed the Thirteenth Amendment, which abolished slavery, an action that had come at Lincoln's urging. He had told the representatives and senators in his annual message, "The voice of the people [had been] heard upon the question," and he wanted abolition made complete, legal, and universal. It was reported that Lincoln "thought this measure was a very fitting if not an indispensable adjunct to winding up of the great difficulty." By the day of his inauguration, seventeen states had already ratified the amendment, and by December 18, 1865, twenty-seven states had approved it, thus making it law.[5]

Fourth, the administration was receiving signals indicating that some leaders of the Confederacy were eager for peace. Conditions in the South were desperate, with shortages of food and supplies, staggering military losses, little hope of foreign aid, and low morale in the army and among the citizens. Some states were withholding their support of the Confederate government. Lincoln and Seward had held an unsuccessful but revealing four-hour informal conference with rebel commissioners Alexander Stephens, R. M. T. Hunter, and John A. Campbell at Hampton Roads on February 3, 1865, to discuss the possible cessation of military activities. But at the moment, the Confederates were unwilling to meet Lincoln's three peace conditions: the restoration of national authority, the acceptance of the Union position on slavery, and the disbanding of all hostile forces. Upon

3. Benjamin P. Thomas, *Abraham Lincoln: A Biography* (New York, 1952), 452–53; Roy P. Basler (ed.), *The Collected Works of Abraham Lincoln* (9 vols.; New Brunswick, N.J., 1953), VIII, 149–50.

4. Basler (ed.), *Collected Works*, VIII, 148.

5. *Ibid.*, VIII, 254; John G. Nicolay and John Hay, *Abraham Lincoln: A History* (10 vols.; New York, 1904), X, 72–90.

learning about the developments at the conference, Jefferson Davis lashed out before cheering Confederates at a mass meeting, swearing that he would "compel the Yankees, in less than twelve months to petition us for peace on our own terms." He stated that before the campaign was over, "His Majesty Abraham the First" and Seward might find "they had been speaking to their masters." Davis, by his extravagant rhetoric, stood in the way of other southerners who recognized that continuation of the conflict was hopeless, but the Confederate president was losing his hold on his Congress and his people. Two days before the inauguration Lincoln received more encouraging news. General Robert E. Lee had written to Grant, proposing to meet him, "with the hope that upon an interchange of views it may be found practicable to submit the subjects of controversy between the belligerents to a convention" to adjust "the present unhappy difficulties." Lincoln continued to maintain the attitude that he had expressed earlier about peace overtures, telling Grant, "Let nothing which is transpiring change, hinder, or delay your military movements or plans."[6]

The Second Inaugural Address, sometimes called Lincoln's Sermon on the Mount, was a concise, tightly constructed composition that did not waste words on ceremonial niceties or superficial sentiment. The shortest presidential inaugural address up to that time, it was only 700 words long, compared to 3,700 words for the First, and required from 5 to 7 minutes to deliver. In four paragraphs consisting of twenty-five sentences, Lincoln attempted to answer the question of why the war came. The opening paragraph dealt with the present and dismissed the necessity of a long speech and a review of the state of the war — "the progress of our arms . . . is . . . well known to the public." The second paragraph, equally short, was a narration of the origin of the war. The third, the body of the speech, philosophized on why a "Living God" gave "to both North and South this terrible war." The concluding fourth paragraph, looking to the future, was an exhortation — "Let us strive on to finish the work we are in." Lord Charnwood said of it, "Probably no other speech of a modern statesman" used "so unreservedly the language of intense religious feeling."[7]

6. Nicolay and Hay, *Abraham Lincoln*, X, 113–31; Basler (ed.), *Collected Works*, VIII, 258, 274–85.

7. *Lincoln Lore*, No. 1226 (October 6, 1952), and No. 1352 (March 7, 1955); Lord Charnwood, *Abraham Lincoln* (New York, 1917), 439.

Unfortunately, Lincoln left no account of how or when he prepared this address. The sole reference by F. B. Carpenter suggested that Lincoln had a draft perhaps a week before he delivered the speech. The internal structure offers evidence that he had reflected on some of the ideas since the outbreak of hostilities and that some passages had been paraphrased from earlier occasions. The address stands as the final crystallization of his philosophical and theological interpretation of the role of a "Living God" in the affairs of man.[8]

Internally, the Second Inaugural Address indicates that Lincoln had at least three major objectives on March 4. On the practical side, Lincoln made an appeal to his countrymen to finish the war without compromise or halfhearted measures. He was speaking to northerners who were tired of the war and its sacrifices, and at the same time he was attempting to answer those peace Democrats who had backed McClellan in the recent election and had advocated a negotiated settlement. He was attempting to counter well-meaning schemes to sidetrack the war by uniting the two sides against a common enemy such as Mexico. Perhaps he was thinking about the efforts of Francis P. Blair, Sr., who had actually made such a proposal to Jefferson Davis. Lincoln may have recalled what Alexander Stephens had suggested at the Hampton Roads conference: "Both parties might for a while leave their present strife in abeyance and occupy themselves with some continental question till their anger should cool and accommodation become possible." Lincoln had told Blair and Stephens that he would have no part in these schemes to divert attention from the real issues—a lasting peace and complete abolition of slavery.[9]

Another part of Lincoln's direct appeal was his hope to keep the momentum going among the states to ratify the Thirteenth Amendment. Furthermore, he made ratification a condition of reentry into the Union.

A second objective of immediate import was to convey his attitudes to those insurgents wavering at the moment over whether to continue the war. Lincoln surmised that people in North Carolina and Georgia might listen, for their governors had refused to cooperate with the authorities in Richmond. In an attempt to make return to the Union as unembarrassing as possible, Lincoln strove to suggest that he was charitable, moderate, and fair. He minimized differences, made no

8. F. B. Carpenter, *Six Months at the White House* (New York, 1867), 234.
9. Nicolay and Hay, *Abraham Lincoln*, X, 119.

mention of the Confederacy, which he had never recognized, did not speak of enemies or rebels or Confederate armies, and refused to indulge in extravagant claims about the Union armies, simply saying that their progress was "reasonably satisfactory and encouraging to all." He hoped that southerners would respond to his concession that both North and South shared responsibility for the conflict and for slavery—"let us judge not, that we be not judged"—and to his closing plea for "malice toward none . . . charity for all."

Taking a stance similar to that in the First Inaugural Address, Lincoln continued to direct attention away from his own role. He used the third-person point of view, speaking in the first person only once. He tried to avoid emotionally loaded terms, referring instead to progress of our arms, insurgent agents, the conflict, the nation's wounds, and a lasting peace.

In the speech, Lincoln made no attempt to appease radical Republicans bent upon revenge, abolitionists determined to scourge southerners for slavery, or disgruntled Democrats eager to defeat the Thirteenth Amendment. How different the language and manner of Lincoln were from the attitudes of those who were soon to wave the bloody shirt.

Lincoln's third objective, expressed in the long third paragraph, was to interpret the deeper meaning of the great conflict for devout and thoughtful persons who, like himself, had agonized over the staggering sacrifices and suffered torment over the question of why a "Living God" had not seemed to answer their prayers. This part of the speech seemed to confirm Nathaniel Wright Stephenson's belief that Lincoln breathed "a lofty confidence as if his soul was gazing meditatively downward upon life, and upon his work, from a secure height." Lincoln seemed to detach himself from immediate decisions and move away from his daily frustrations in an attempt to touch upon the innermost feelings of perplexed citizens. Much like a pastor, he spoke from a biblical text: "Woe unto the world because of offenses, for it must need be that offenses come, but woe to that man by whom the offense cometh" (Matt. 18:7). In his tightly constructed sentences that drew much from the Scriptures for language and authority, Lincoln expressed what the Quaker philosopher Elton Trueblood has called a "theology of anguish." The address revealed Lincoln's search for the will of the "Living God." Trueblood shows that Lincoln's theology, growing out of many years of reading the Bible, had found frequent expression in his letters and speeches since 1862.[10]

The basic statement of the third paragraph is devoted to what Trueblood termed "a theological analysis of the conflict." Its implications can be fathomed when one considers it in four parts, involving cause, result, interpretation, and amplification.[11]

In the opening four sentences Lincoln pointed to the differences over slavery as the cause of the war.

One eighth of the whole population were colored slaves, not distributed generally over the Union, but localized in the Southern part of it. These slaves constituted a peculiar and powerful interest. All knew that this interest was, somehow, the cause of the war. To strengthen, perpetuate, and extend this interest was the object for which the insurgents would rend the Union, even by war; while the government claimed no right to do more than to restrict the territorial enlargement of it.

In the second part of the paragraph, Lincoln declared the results of each side's praying to the same God.

Neither party expected for the war the magnitude or the duration which it has already attained. Neither anticipated that the cause of the conflict might cease with or even before the conflict itself should cease. Each looked for an easier triumph, and a result less fundamental and astounding. Both read the same Bible and pray to the same God, and each invokes His aid against the other. It may seem strange that any men should dare to ask a just God's assistance in wringing their bread from the sweat of other men's faces [Gen. 3:19], but let us judge not, that we be not judged [Matt. 7:1]. The prayers of both could not be answered; that of neither has been answered fully.

In the third part Lincoln came to the heart of his theological interpretation, saying that God had punished both North and South for the war.

The Almighty has His own purposes. "Woe unto the world because of offenses; for it must needs be that offenses come; but woe to that man by whom the offense cometh" [Matt. 18:7]. If we shall suppose that American slavery is one of those offenses which, in the providence of God, must needs come, but which, having continued through His appointed time, He now wills to remove, and that He gives to both North and South this terrible war,

10. Nathaniel Wright Stephenson, *Lincoln* (Indianapolis, 1922), 405–406. All excerpts from the Second Inaugural Address are taken from Basler (ed.), *Collected Works*, VIII, 332–33. Elton Trueblood, *Abraham Lincoln: Theologian of American Anguish* (New York, 1973), 135–41.

11. Basler (ed.), *Collected Works*, VIII, 332–33. See also *Lincoln Lore*, No. 1226.

as the woe due to those by whom the offense came, shall we discern therein any departure from those divine attributes which the believers in a Living God always ascribe to Him?

Concluding his analysis in the fourth part, Lincoln amplified his theology and affirmed his faith in "the judgments of the Lord."

Fondly do we hope, fervently do we pray, that this mighty scourge of war may speedily pass away. Yet, if God wills that it continue, until all the wealth piled by the bondsman's two hundred and fifty years of unrequited toil shall be sunk, and until every drop of blood drawn with the lash, shall be paid by another drawn with the sword, as was said three thousand years ago, so still it must be said, "the judgments of the Lord, are true and righteous altogether" [Ps. 19:9].

The theology can be summarized in three basic propositions that emerge: "In the providence of God," American slavery ("two hundred and fifty years of unrequited toil") was an "offense"; a "Living God" gave to "both North and South this terrible war" as punishment; and God willed that war continue until the offense was paid for.

At the heart of Lincoln's argument was a discernible categorical syllogism, but as a skillful communicator, he presented his propositions in enthymematic form. Lincoln probably hoped his listeners would recognize the analogy between the punishment of Israelites sent to Babylon and Americans who permitted slavery to continue for 250 years. For those indoctrinated in Protestant theology, particularly Calvinists and Baptists, who accepted without question the proposition that God punished the sinful, Lincoln had provided a way to rationalize the pain and suffering of the war. In a letter to Thurlow Weed, Lincoln explained his strategy: "Men are not flattered by being shown that there has been a difference of purpose between the Almighty and them. To deny it, however, in this case is to deny that there is a God governing the world."[12]

An intriguing question is whether Lincoln thought he could appeal to fundamentalist Christians in the South, who were more devout than were many of their northern brothers. In 1865, most southerners would not have granted Lincoln his premise that slavery was a sin, but they would have been fully in accord with the assertion that God controlled the affairs of man and punished sinners. The reality of defeat was a severe blow to southern self-esteem. It was not long before

12. Abraham Lincoln to Thurlow Weed, March 15, 1865, in Basler (ed.), *Collected Works*, VIII, 356.

southern preachers were drawing parallels between the Crucifixion and the South's loss of the war, which they called God's test of their faith.

Abraham Lincoln, at this most eloquent moment in his career, did not indulge in a persuasion that depended upon the hard sell or that sought to exploit bitter emotions. Instead, this leader who had come through fire pursued a milder rhetoric steeped in democratic and Christian sentiment. It was a persuasion that sought identification with simple, God-fearing citizens of his time and of the future. Perhaps for this reason, the Second Inaugural Address is revered by freedom lovers everywhere.

VIII

"PENETRATING AND FAR-REACHING"

Lincoln's Voice

Louis A. Warren's *Lincoln's Gettysburg Declaration: A New Birth of Freedom* is detailed and exhaustive in its analysis of the contributing factors, the speech preparation, the occasion, the sources of the ideas and language, the holographs, and the immediate and subsequent reactions. But the book, like many others, gives scant attention to what Warren refers to in one place as "the President's vibrant voice," disposing of the topic in one short paragraph of fewer than two hundred words and five other scattered references. His citations are limited to descriptions consisting of a sentence or less by three earwitnesses, two of whom are unidentified, and four reminiscences made long after the event.[1]

My present purpose is not to disparage the scholarship of Warren, who was resourceful in locating as much as he did. More properly, Warren's treatment of Lincoln's voice is mentioned to illustrate how little is known about the subject. Reporters of the nineteenth century had difficulty describing any voice in meaningful terms. A photograph can clarify a comment about gesture and posture; but without a recording, a reporter can seldom suggest through words "the sound of a voice that is still."

Perhaps a review of what little is available concerning Lincoln's voice will expose myth, fiction, and ignorance. A search of the literature reveals that those who actually heard Lincoln rarely devoted much more than a sentence to the subject of his voice. What they said often reflects both their own political bias and the journalistic excesses of the day. For example, in 1848 the *Bristol County Democrat* (Taunton, Mass.) described Lincoln. "His awkward gesticulation, the

---

1. Louis A. Warren, *Lincoln's Gettysburg Declaration: A New Birth of Freedom* (Fort Wayne, Ind., 1964), 110, 120, 122, 123, 127. When he dealt with the same subject earlier, in *Lincoln Lore*, No. 340 (October 14, 1935), Warren was equally limited in firsthand evidence and quoted excerpts from statements of eight unidentified earwitnesses.

ludicrous management of his voice and the comical expression of his countenance, all conspired to make his hearers laugh at the mere anticipation of the joke before it appeared."[2]

In spite of the fact that the Lincoln-Douglas Debates of 1858 were more fully reported than were any other controversies of the day, accounts included only occasional references to Lincoln's vocal quality. On June 15, 1858, a correspondent for the New York *Tribune* characterized Lincoln as "colloquial, affable, good natured, almost jolly. . . . He was simply talking about things as they are, in a pleasant after dinner mood." On August 25, 1858, another reporter observed that "Mr. Lincoln spoke about two hours in an earnest, calm, convincing manner." In reporting the Quincy debate, a correspondent concluded that "almost everybody present could hear Mr. Lincoln distinctly and not a hundred in the crowd could understand Mr. Douglas."[3]

On a side trip, when Lincoln paused briefly in Burlington, Iowa, the editor of the Burlington *Hawk-Eye* recorded that he "appeared . . . fresh and vigorous, there was nothing in his voice, manner or appearance to show the arduous labor of the last two months. . . . In this respect he had altogether the advantage of Douglas, whose voice is cracked and husky, temper soured and general appearance denoting exhaustion."[4]

When Lincoln appeared at a Republican mass meeting in Cincinnati in 1859, a reporter mentioned that he spoke "with singular clearness of enunciation and deliberation, duly punctuating every sentence as he uttered it. The people were satisfied with the voice . . . and listened expectantly."[5]

The Beloit *Journal* of October 19, 1859, printed a short article entitled "A Portrait of 'Abe' Lincoln" by "the spicy correspondent of the *Oconto* [Wisconsin] *Pioneer*." This observer remarked that Lincoln's voice was "not heavy, but it has a clear trumpet tone that can be heard an immense distance. Except N. P. Banks, I have never heard a man who could talk to a large crowd with such ease." The reporter

2. Roy P. Basler (ed.), *The Collected Works of Abraham Lincoln* (9 vols.; New Brunswick, N.J., 1953), II, 7.

3. Herbert Mitgang (ed.), *Lincoln As They Saw Him* (New York, 1959), 96–98; Chicago *Press and Tribune*, August 28, 1858; Unnamed source quoted in *Lincoln Lore*, No. 340 (October 14, 1935).

4. Burlington (Iowa) *Hawk-Eye*, October 11, 1858, quoted in Ben Hur Wilson, "Lincoln at Burlington," *Palimpsest*, XXIV (October, 1943), 321.

5. Cincinnati *Daily Commercial*, September 19, 1859.

apparently heard Lincoln in person, but he did not reveal what the occasion was. The emphasis on the carrying power of Lincoln's voice was significant.

What impression did Lincoln make when he spoke to the sophisticated New York audience at Cooper Union? The New York *Herald* described his voice as "sharp and powerful at times" but having "a frequent tendency to dwindle into a shrill and unpleasant sound. His enunciation is slow and emphatic." Perhaps there was much truth in one reporter's reaction that "the tones, the gestures, the kindling eye and the mirth-provoking look, defy the reporter's skill."[6]

There are comments difficult to associate with a given occasion. The New York *Tribune* of November 10, 1860, stated that "his utterance is peculiarly assured and emphatic." The New York *World* referred to his voice in 1860 as "soft and sympathetic as a girl's. Although not lifted above a tone of average conversation, it was distinctly audible throughout the entire hall."[7]

A reporter thought that the First Inaugural Address "was delivered in a clear and emphatic voice, which never faltered throughout, and reached nearly to the outskirts of the vast throng." The same observer wrote that Lincoln read his message in a "loud clear voice."[8] The Cincinnati *Daily Commercial* of November 23, 1863, described Lincoln's voice at Gettysburg as "sharp, unmusical, and treble."

Although accounts of earwitnesses are difficult to find, it is not difficult to locate reminiscences that refer to Lincoln's voice. The reliability of these memories is impossible to assess. Perhaps the person who had the most opportunities to hear Lincoln on a variety of occasions, at least before his presidency, was William Herndon. In answer to an inquiry, Herndon wrote in 1887 that "Lincoln's voice was when he first began speaking, shrill-squeaking-piping, unpleasant. . . . As Mr. Lincoln proceeded further along with his oration . . . he gently and gradually warmed up—his shrill-squeaking-piping voice became harmonious, melodious—musical, if you please."[9]

In 1908, Horace White recalled hearing Lincoln at Springfield on

6. New York *Herald*, February 28, 1860; New York *Tribune*, February 28, 1860.
7. Mitgang (ed.), *Lincoln*, 202; Henry Clay Whitney, *Life on the Circuit with Lincoln* (Caldwell, Idaho, 1940), 199.
8. New York *Daily Tribune*, March 5, 1861.
9. William Herndon to Truman H. Bartlett, July 19, 1887, in Massachusetts Historical Society, Boston. This is essentially the same quotation found in William H. Herndon and Jesse William Weik, *Herndon's Lincoln* (Springfield, Ill., 1930) 331–33.

October 4, 1854. White remembered that Lincoln "began in a slow and hesitating manner, but without any mistakes of language, dates, or facts. . . . He had a thin, high-pitched falsetto voice of much carrying power, that could be heard a long distance in spite of the bustle and tumult of a crowd. He had the accent and pronunciation peculiar to his native state, Kentucky." During the Lincoln-Douglas Debates, White accompanied Lincoln throughout Illinois. In an address in 1914, White described Lincoln in Ottawa: "Lincoln began to speak in a slow and rather awkward way. He had a thin tenor, or rather falsetto voice, almost as high pitched as a boatswain's whistle. It could be heard farther and it had better wearing qualities than Douglas' rich baritone, but it was not so impressive to the listeners."[10]

Thomas Drummond, a judge on the United States District Court during the last ten years of Lincoln's law practice, described his voice as "by no means pleasing, and, indeed, when excited, in its shrill tones sometimes almost disagreeable." Well after the turn of the century, Carl Schurz remembered Lincoln's speaking at Quincy in 1858: "His voice was not musical rather high-keyed and apt to turn into a shrill treble in moments of excitement; but it was not positively disagreeable. It had an exceedingly penetrating, far-reaching quality. The looks of the audience convinced me that every word he spoke was understood at the remotest edges of the vast assemblage." Chauncey M. Depew wrote almost fifty years after the war, "In speaking Mr. Lincoln had a peculiar cadence in his voice, caused by laying emphasis upon the key-word of the sentence." John G. Nicolay, in discussing the Cooper Union speech, spoke of "the clear ring of his rather high-pitched voice." Noah Brooks recalled: "Lincoln's voice was not sonorous, and at times it rose to a high somewhat shrill key. In ordinary conversation his tones were agreeable, and his enunciation clear. When excited, in speaking, he rose to a commanding height."[11]

Many people remembered Lincoln's delivery of the First Inaugural Address. In recounting that occasion, Nicolay said, "As Lincoln's voice, trained to open-air speaking, rang out, clear and resonant,

10. Horace White, "Abraham Lincoln in 1854," *Transactions of the Illinois State Historical Society*, 1908, No. 13 (1909), 32; Horace White, *Lincoln and Douglas Debates, An Address Before The Chicago Historical Society, February 7, 1914* (Chicago, Illinois, 1914), 20.

11. Francis Fisher Browne, *Everyday Life of Abraham Lincoln* (New York, 1887), 142–43; Carl Schurz, *Reminiscences of Carl Schurz, 1852–1863* (2 vols.; New York, 1909), II, 93; Depew, *My Memories*, 57–58; John G. Nicolay, *A Short Life of Abraham Lincoln* (New York, 1902), 38; Noah Brooks, *Life of Lincoln* (New York, 1888), 129.

above the vast throngs of people before him, the feelings of those who heard him were deeply stirred." Brooks eloquently recorded that the inaugural address "was received with almost profound silence. Every word was clear and audible as the somewhat shrill and ringing tones of Lincoln's voice sounded over the vast concourse." James Grant Wilson said that Lincoln read "in a strong high-pitched voice, what he believed to be the best of all his oratorical efforts." George W. Julian, a congressman from Indiana, remembered that "his voice, though not very strong or full-toned, rang out over the acres of people before him with surprising distinctness, and, I think, was heard in the remotest part of his audience."[12]

William E. Barton collected an interesting set of reminiscences for his book *Lincoln at Gettysburg*. He included a statement made in May, 1885, by Andrew G. Curtin, governor of Pennsylvania at the time of the dedication. "He pronounced that speech in a voice that all the multitude heard." Horatio King reports that he took down the governor's exact words in an interview.[13]

Frequently cited as an excellent description is that by P. M. Bikle, Dean Emeritus of Gettysburg College and head of the Latin Department for forty-five years, who heard the address when he was a college sophomore. He reminisced: "He spoke in a most deliberate manner, and with such a forceful and articulate expression that he could be heard by all of that immense throng. It is seldom I have heard any one whose voice carried so well." H. C. Holloway said: "His clear ringing voice carried his words all over that vast assembly. As the President began to speak I instinctively felt that the occasion was taking on a new grandeur, as of a great moment in history, and then there followed, in slow, clear and most impressive far-reaching utterance the words with which the whole world has long since been familiar."[14]

Henry E. Jacobs, a student at the Lutheran Theological Seminary at the time of the address, remembered, "There was something so unusual in the tones of his voice and in his mode of address, that long

12. Nicolay, *Short Life*, 243; Noah Brooks, "Lincoln's Reelection" *Century Magazine*, XL (April, 1895), 871–77; Allen Thorndike Rice (ed.), *Reminiscences of Abraham Lincoln by Distinguished Men of His Time* (New York, 1886), 30, 50.

13. William E. Barton, *Lincoln at Gettysburg* (Indianapolis, 1930), 167; Horatio King, *Turning on the Light* (Philadelphia, 1895), 238.

14. Philip M. Bikle (Typescript in Civil War Collections, Gettysburg College Library, Gettysburg); Barton, *Lincoln at Gettysburg*, 181.

before those present were ready to weigh his words he had finished." Wilson reported that "the immense audience that was within the sound of his strong tenor and far-reaching voice listened almost breathlessly during its delivery." On February 12, 1915, Joseph A. Gouldon recounted: "He began his speech in clear, distinct tones that carried to quite a distance. At first his voice trembled slightly, but speedily recovered, and amid a profound silence the audience heard the words that were uttered by President Lincoln." In August, 1917, Joseph L. Gilbert, a newspaperman who had reported the address, said, "His marvelous voice, careering in fullness of utterance and clearness of tone, was perfectly audible on the outskirts of the crowd." Oliver Goldsmith, who had guarded the president, recalled after fifty years that "Lincoln's deep powerful voice could be heard by everyone."[15]

Barton reported from memory a statement by S. S. Warner, who mentioned "the high pitch and thin quality of his voice" but said that "he was heard distinctly." Barton also quoted Clark E. Carr, who recalled that Lincoln "began in those high clarion tones which the people of Illinois had so often heard, to which he said to the close. His was a voice that, when he made an effort, could reach a great multitude, and he always tried to make everyone hear."[16]

The author certainly does not claim to have located all references to Lincoln's voice, but, of what remains for the biographers to base their descriptions upon, he has attempted to provide a representative selection. Casual listeners suggest that Lincoln's voice was high-pitched and at times unpleasant but that it had carrying power.

None of the earwitnesses set out to give a complete description of how Lincoln sounded, and their evaluations were usually incidental to their reporting of what he said. In contrast, the reminiscences are much fuller and more specific in their characterizations. Herndon, White, Drummond, Brooks, and Schurz were in essential agreement that at times Lincoln's voice was "by no means pleasing." The most

15. Barton, *Lincoln at Gettysburg*, 184, 187, 188; Address delivered at National Shorthand Recorders' Association, August, 1917, in Barton, *Lincoln at Gettysburg*, 189; Chicago *Journal*, November 19, 1913, in Barton, *Lincoln at Gettysburg*, 192.

16. Barton says, "I give from memory the story of the Gettysburg Address as I heard it from the Honorable S. S. Warner, at one time State Treasurer of Ohio" (Barton, *Lincoln at Gettysburg*, 192). Colonel Carr "who represented Illinois on the Gettysburg Cemetery Commission, and who sat near to Mr. Lincoln as he delivered his address related the story of the occasion" (Barton, *Lincoln at Gettysburg*, 202).

troublesome terms are the following: shrill-squeaking-piping (Herndon), falsetto voice (White), shrill tones (Drummond), shrill treble (Schurz), and shrill key (Brooks). It is indeed disturbing to associate these descriptions with a man who was reportedly an effective stump speaker as well as a successful lawyer and the orator who produced the Gettysburg Address.

The Barton collection, on the whole, shows a different emphasis and reflects the tendency to create a favorable image of a hero. Bikle spoke of Lincoln's "forceful and articulate expression"; Holloway used the words "clear ringing voice"; Jacobs recalled "something so unusual in the tones of his voice"; Wilson called it a "strong tenor . . . voice"; Gilbert thought the right adjective was "marvelous"; Goldsmith called it a "deep powerful voice"; and Carr spoke of his "high clarion tones." These evaluations are easier to accept because they permit a more favorable connotation, but they tell us almost nothing about the vocal quality of the flesh-and-blood Lincoln.

Those who heard Lincoln could have most easily made judgments about his loudness and about whether he could be heard. They certainly could have decided whether they considered his voice pleasant or unpleasant. Why only one observer classified Lincoln's voice as tenor is indeed puzzling. But judgments about its pitch and quality—whether it was falsetto, shrill, or treble—were probably subjective. Those who have reminisced about Lincoln undoubtedly repeated each other. Instead of remembering what they actually heard, they strove to express in other words what someone else had said.

This study suggests that little of a dependable nature remains concerning Lincoln's voice. The earwitnesses have left only fragmentary reports, and the reminiscences, made long after Lincoln's death, are open to serious question. But it is upon these scraps and pieces that the biographers have relied.

In spite of the dearth of information on the subject, many Americans today believe that they know how Lincoln sounded. The voices of actors and readers such as Raymond Massey have become a significant part of the Lincoln myth. Massey wrote regarding his interpretation, "As far as I know Mr. Lincoln's voice was high pitched and shrill, which would account for the fact that he could address thousands of people quite audibly, but I considered that for dramatic purposes a deeper register was more effective, even though it had no authenticity."[17] The speaking figures of Lincoln in the Illinois State Pavilion at the New York World's Fair and at Disneyland have further added to the myth. The voice of Lincoln in these exhibits is that of motion picture and television personality Royal Dano.[18]

17. Raymond Massey, *The Writings and Speeches of Abraham Lincoln*, 1961; Raymond Massey to the author, May 12, 1964.
18. Robert Jackson, Public Relations Director, WED Enterprises, Inc., to the author, May 28, 1965.

IX

"A WESTERN MAN"
Lincoln's Appearance and Delivery

Curiosity about Abraham Lincoln is insatiable. People have inquired about such personal details as his daily routine, hair, exact measurements, reading habits, purchases at the local store, bank deposits, love affairs, marital life, churchgoing, mental health, and diseases. Friends, mere acquaintances, and even some casual observers have produced reminiscences, detailing memories, opinions, and hearsay. And what they could not remember they simply made up, or they repeated what others had said. In addition, some of our best scholars and writers have interpreted and reinterpreted Lincoln and his times in monographs, biographies, and historical works.

In spite of this outpouring of material, writers have given comparatively little attention to Lincoln's platform delivery, a significant aspect of his immediate effectiveness. No doubt Lincoln established rapport with his listeners through his appearance, facial expression, voice, and the other nuances that hold people's attention and fascinate authors. Much of what we know comes from recollections made many years after his assassination. As a result, we have either a mythical Lincoln or what J. G. Randall once called a "second hand description."[1]

In the previous chapter discussing Abraham Lincoln's voice, I drew mainly upon the reports of earwitnesses. Similarly, in this discussion of his appearance and delivery, I shall confine my sources as much as possible to eyewitnesses and to those who knew him personally.[2]

What do the 120 known photographs and the statues reveal about the speaking of Abraham Lincoln? What remain are posed figures, seated or standing in fixed positions to accommodate the crude camera exposures. In some the head is probably held rigid by an "immobilizer," a torturous metal bracket. The 31 photographers exercised little variation in positioning their subject. Often they presented either

1. James G. Randall, *Lincoln, the President* (4 vols.; New York, 1945–55), III, 394.
2. Paul M. Angle wrote, "Not many men knew Lincoln well and of those who did only six — Herndon, Lamon, Whitney, Arnold, Nicolay and Hay — wrote extensively of his life" ("Introduction" to Henry Clay Whitney, *Life on the Circuit with Lincoln* [Caldwell, Idaho, 1940], 19).

a full-figured Lincoln standing bolt upright with his hand resting on a table or a seated Lincoln in a formal chair with his hand in his lap or on a table. The Lincoln photographs show the same stiffness of pose as do those of other public figures of the time.

All the photographs but three show Lincoln with his hair nicely combed, parted, and often slicked down. But people in Illinois were not accustomed to seeing the well-coiffed figure in the photographs. More likely they saw "his thick, coarse and defiant" hair standing "out in every direction." Ward Lamon called it "stiff and unkempt." When he made Lincoln's life mask, Leonard W. Volk recalled that "his long dark hair [stood] out at every imaginable angle, apparently uncombed for a week."[3]

Although they give some notion of Lincoln's general appearance and clothing, there is another reason the pictures must be discounted. Lincoln usually dressed up for the sittings, and the photographers often straightened his clothing to get what they considered the best visual effect. One eager photographer who pulled Lincoln off the street lent him a coat, and Mathew Brady adjusted Lincoln's collar to shorten his neck. About 80 of the 120 known pictures show Lincoln with a beard, wearing formal clothing. But not one gives us any hint about the Lincoln who traveled the circuit or faced rallies in rural Illinois.[4]

Because his first picture was made in 1847, when he was thirty-seven years old, we have little idea about the appearance of the younger Lincoln who lived in New Salem and served four terms in the Illinois legislature. The expressions in the pictures taken before 1860 are impassive, somber, and sometimes almost lifeless. In the photographs taken after 1860 the strain of being president is reflected in tiredness, sadness, and even remorsefulness. His eyes seem curiously indifferent or reveal a faraway stare. Among the likenesses, only one shows the slightest hint of a smile. Walt Whitman concluded: "None of the artists or pictures has caught the deep, though subtle and indirect expression of this man's face. There is something else there."[5]

3. Lew Wallace, *An Autobiography* (2 vols.; New York, 1876), I, 222; Ward Lamon, *Life of Abraham Lincoln* (Boston, 1872), 469; Leonard W. Volk, "The Lincoln Life-Mask and How It Was Made," *Century Magazine*, XXIII (December, 1881), 225. Lincoln approved a photograph with mussed hair (Alexander Hesler photograph taken February 28, 1857). Lincoln to James F. Babcock, September 13, 1860, in Roy P. Basler (ed.), *The Collected Works of Abraham Lincoln* (9 vols.; New Brunswick, N.J., 1953), IV, 114.
4. Stefan Lorant, *Lincoln: A Picture Story of His Life* (New York, 1952), 96–97.
5. Charles Hamilton and Lloyd Ostendorf, *Lincoln in Photographs: An Album of Every*

The statues, most in marble or bronze, are no more helpful in revealing the speaking Lincoln than are the photographs. Only three of the sculptors had any direct contact with the man, and of these only Vinnie Ream observed Lincoln at work. The others relied upon pictures, engravings, or imagination. Not until after 1880 did they have available the Volk life mask prepared in 1860. The statues showed Lincoln on horseback, wielding an axe, gesturing, or orating. The majority of the sculptors produced a bearded Lincoln standing with his hands at his sides or behind him. The famous statue in the Lincoln Memorial in Washington, D.C., depicts him seated in a great chair.[6]

Contemporary testimony suggests that Lincoln gave a negative first impression. Eyewitnesses generally described him as dark complexioned, dark visaged, and swarthy. Ward Lamon said that "his complexion was very dark, his skin yellow, shrivelled and 'leathery.'" The poet Edwin Markham said, "The color of the ground was in him, the red earth; / The smack and tang of elemental things."[7]

The New York journalist Henry Villard said Lincoln was "undescribably gawky." Another journalist, Donn Piatt, concluded that Lincoln was "the homeliest man" he had ever seen. One who observed Lincoln just before his inauguration conceded, "He is . . . not so bad looking as they say while he is no great beauty." Another concurred, saying that he was "not so ugly as he is generally represented."[8]

In 1860 a London journalist saw in Lincoln "an honest old lawyer, with a face half Roman, half Indian, wasted by climate, scarred by life's struggles." It took Walt Whitman to penetrate the subtlety of Lincoln's visage. After observing the president in the streets of Washington, the poet referred to Lincoln as "a Hoosier Michael Angelo, so awfully ugly" that his face became "beautiful with its strange mouth, its deep cut, criss-cross lines and its doughnut complexion." In his face and general appearance Lincoln showed the results of rough

Known Pose (Norman, Okla., 1963), Chaps. 9–10; Frederick Meserve and Carl Sandburg, *The Photographs of Abraham Lincoln* (New York, 1944); Louis Untermeyer (ed.), *The Poetry and Prose of Walt Whitman* (New York, 1949), 627.

6. F. Lauriston Bullard, *Lincoln in Marble and Bronze* (New Brunswick, N.J., 1952), 4–5.

7. Lamon, *Life of Lincoln*, 469; Edwin Markham, "Lincoln, the Man of the People," in Edward Wagenknecht (ed.), *Abraham Lincoln* (New York, 1947), 604–605.

8. Harold G. Villard and Oswald Garrison Villard (eds.), *Lincoln on the Eve of '61* (New York, 1961), 3; Donn Piatt, *Memories of the Men Who Saved the Union* (New York, 1887), 24; George C. Shepard to Mr. and Mrs. Lucius M. Boltwood, February 21, 1861, Adoniran J. Blakely to Dan Blakely, February 18, 1861, both in Harry E. Pratt, *Concerning Lincoln* (Springfield, Ill., 1944), 56, 53.

living—flatboating, surveying, riding horseback, and traveling the circuit—in frontier Illinois.[9]

William Herndon gives us a view of Lincoln in action, particularly with reference to posture and gesture. In 1887 he recalled:

When he rose to speak to the jury or to crowds of people, he stood inclined forward, was awkward, angular, ungainly, odd. . . . As he proceeded in his address, he used his hands—especially and generally his right hand—in his gestures; he used his head a great deal in speaking, throwing or jerking or moving it now here and now there, now in this position and now in that, in order to be more emphatic, to drive the idea home. Mr. Lincoln never beat the air; never sawed space with his hands, never acted for stage effect. . . . Bear in mind that he did not gesticulate much and yet it is true that every organ of his body was in motion and acted with ease, elegance, and grace. . . . When Mr. Lincoln rose up to speak, he rose slowly, steadily, firmly; he never moved much about on the stand or platform when speaking, trusting no desk, table, railing; he ran his eyes slowly over the crowd. . . . In his greatest inspiration he held both of his hands out above his head at an angle of about fifty degrees, hands open or clenched, according to his feeling and his ideas.[10]

Perhaps the element of his appearance that received the most comment was Lincoln's body structure. He was about 6 feet 4 inches tall and weighed about 180 pounds. To describe him, observers used such words as not muscular, wiry, rawboned, tall, gaunt, awkward, ill-proportioned, and ungainly. John G. Nicolay described his "thin, but sinewy neck, rather long; long arms; large hands; chest thin and narrow as compared with his great height; legs of more than proportionate length and large feet." His leanness probably seemed even more pronounced because his coat sleeves and pants were usually too short. A stovepipe hat made him tower over his companions. Lincoln's size was particularly noticeable when he appeared on the platform in 1858 with the Little Giant, Douglas, who was a foot shorter.[11]

Undoubtedly his height, slenderness, and clothing gave Lincoln an ungainly appearance. Many observers commented on his awkwardness. Whitney said that his gestures were "angular and eccentric." Schurz reported that "he swung his long arms sometimes in a very

9. Hamilton and Ostendorf, *Lincoln in Photographs*, 52; Emory Holloway (ed.), *Uncollected Poetry and Prose of Walt Whitman* (2 vols.; New York, 1932), II, 23.
10. William Herndon to Truman Bartlett, July 19, 1887, in Massachusetts Historical Society, Boston.
11. Lincoln to Jesse W. Fell, December 20, 1859, in Basler (ed.), *Collected Works*, III, 512; John G. Nicolay, "Lincoln's Personal Appearance," *Century Magazine*, XLII (October, 1891), 932.

ungraceful manner. Now and then he would, to give particular emphasis to a point, bend his knees and body with a sudden downward jerk, and then shoot up again with a vehemence that raised him to his tiptoes and made him look much taller than he really was."[12]

A significant part of Lincoln's rapport with audiences must have come from his expressive face. His longtime friend Joshua Speed said that his countenance indicated that he was "a very sad man." But Speed added that when Lincoln "warmed up all sadness vanished" and his face became "radiant and glowing, and almost gave expression to his thoughts before his tongue could utter them." Piatt wrote: "When in repose, his face was dull, heavy and repellent. It brightened like a lit lantern when animated. His dull eyes would fairly sparkle with fun or express as kindly a look as I ever saw when moved by some matter of human interest."[13]

An observer in 1860 commented that Lincoln's features were "extremely mobile." He contorted his mouth "to provoke uproarious merriment. Good humor [gleams] in his eyes and lurks in the corner of his mouth." Perhaps there is truth in the remark that "so many hard lines in his face" became "a mask of the inner man and his true character only [shone] out when in an animated conversation or when telling an amusing tale."[14]

Whether Lincoln's clothing had any influence upon his Illinois listeners is doubtful. In 1856, Lincoln was described as wearing "a long linen duster, no vest, a pair of low shoes, and brown linen trousers much too abbreviated in their lower extremities to have commanded the approval of a Beau Brummel." The Chicago *Press and Tribune* reported that Lincoln was "never fashionable; he was careless, but not slovenly." Nicolay suggested that when compared to that of many of his associates, Lincoln's appearance was not unusual. "In those days," Nicolay said, "dress was a matter of altogether minor consideration and played an unimportant part as the measure of a man's worth or influence." Further, he explained that anyone "who followed circuit courts from county to county, worrying through snow and mud, fording swollen streams, sleeping on cabin floors, could not

12. Whitney, *Life on the Circuit*, 116; Carl Schurz, *Reminiscences* (2 vols.; New York, 1907–1908), II, 93.

13. Joshua F. Speed, *Reminiscences of Abraham Lincoln* (Louisville, 1884), 34; Piatt, *Memories*, 30.

14. John Henry Brown Journal, August 26, 1860 (Copy in Louis A. Warren Lincoln Library and Museum, Fort Wayne, Ind.).

remain fastidious about costume." Lincoln's slimness and height made it difficult for him to get a good fit in store-bought clothing, which is why his coat sleeves and pants were usually too short.[15]

Did Lincoln's delivery change through the years? Since we have few eyewitness descriptions of Lincoln speaking before 1840, we can only conjecture about how this "rough looking fellow," who had been a store clerk, postmaster, and surveyor, appeared to the citizens of New Salem and the surrounding area. Any descriptions come from reminiscences based upon fading memories by his early acquaintances. Recalling a speech that Lincoln delivered August 4, 1832, Stephen T. Logan said that Lincoln "was a very tall and gawky and rough looking fellow then—his pantaloons didn't meet his shoes by six inches." But after Lincoln began speaking, Logan "became very much interested in him. He made a very sensible speech."[16] In a biography published in 1892, Henry Clay Whitney, who knew Lincoln in the 1850s, recorded, "When he first ran for the legislature he presented this appearance: He wore a blue jeans coat, claw hammer style, short in both the sleeves, and in the tail:—in fact, it was so short in the tail he could not sit on it: homespun linen trousers, a straw hat and 'stogy' boots." Whitney also wrote: "Judge Matheny informs me that when Lincoln first ran for the legislature it was regarded as a joke; the boys wanted some fun: he was so uncouth and awkward, and so illy dressed, that his candidacy afforded a pleasant diversion for them, but it was not expected that it would go any further. It was found, however, during the canvass, that Lincoln knew what he was about and that he had running qualities: so Matheny told him he was sowing seeds of success: and that next year he would win." How much faith can we place in Whitney? In other details about Lincoln, Whitney was not always accurate. He relied on what others had told him, for he did not observe Lincoln in action until after 1850.[17]

We can learn something about the platform manner of Lincoln from the *Illinois State Register*. That paper in 1839 chided Lincoln for "a sort of assumed clownishness. . . . Mr. Lincoln will sometimes

15. D. C. Smith, "The Lincoln Thornton Debate," *Illinois State Historical Society*, X (April, 1917), 98; John L. Scripps, Chicago *Press and Tribune*, May 23, 1860, quoted in Herbert Mitgang (ed.), *Abraham Lincoln: A Press Portrait* (Chicago, 1971), 179; Nicolay, "Lincoln's Personal Appearance," 936.

16. Stephen T. Logan, "Talks About Lincoln," *Bulletin of Abraham Lincoln Association*, Springfield, Illinois, No. 12 (Sept. 1, 1928), 2.

17. Whitney, *Life on the Circuit*, 55–56; in the same volume, see Angle's "Introduction," 19–20.

make his language correspond with his clownish manner, and he can thus frequently raise a loud laugh among his Whig hearers; but this entire game of buffoonery convinces the mind of no man and is utterly lost on the majority of his audience. We seriously advise Mr. Lincoln to correct his clownish fault before it grows upon him." It is entirely likely that "the majority" was largely made up of Democrats. A year later the same newspaper, softening its appraisal, reported that Lincoln "was listened to with attention; possessing much urbanity and suavity . . . he is well calculated for a public debator; as he seldom loses his temper, and always replies jocosely and in good humor, the evident marks of disapprobation which greet many of his assertions, do not discompose him and he is therefore hard to foil."[18]

We have little idea about Lincoln's speaking when he addressed the House of Representatives during his term from 1847 to 1849. In 1848 he campaigned for the Whigs of New England. Concerning his speech at Worcester, Massachusetts, on September 12, 1848, the pro-Whig Boston *Advertiser* reported that Lincoln spoke "in a clear and cool and very eloquent manner." The Boston *Atlas*, on September 16, 1848, declared that his speech was full of "sound reasoning, cogent argument and keen satire" and reported that the Whigs interrupted Lincoln with "rounds of applause." The Whigs of Lowell also appreciated what the reporter called "good sense, sound reasoning, and irresistible argument, spoken with perfect command of manner and matter which so eminently distinguishes Western orators." At Taunton, on September 21, 1848, the Whigs approved of the Illinois representative's presentation. But a reporter with a Democratic bias, granting that Lincoln "believed what he was saying," declared: "The speaker was far inferior as a reasoner to others who hold the same views, but then he was more unscrupulous, more facetious and with his sneers he mixed up a good deal of humor. His awkward gesticulations, the ludicrous management of his voice and the comical expression of his countenance, all conspired to make his hearers laugh at the mere anticipation of the joke before it appeared."[19]

When they referred to Lincoln as a "western man," writers were

---

18. *Illinois State Register* (Springfield, Ill.), November 13, 1839, quoted in Mitgang (ed.), *Press Portrait*, 17–18; the "Patriot," reporting on a speech made at Mount Vernon, Illinois, in *Illinois State Register* (Springfield, Ill.), October 16, 1840, quoted in Earl Schenck Miers (ed.), *Lincoln Day by Day: A Chronology, 1809–1865* (3 vols.; Washington, D.C., 1960), I, 144.

19. Basler (ed.), *Collected Works*, II, 1–7.

attempting to distinguish him from easterners or New Englanders. Isaac Arnold, who knew Lincoln personally, explained:

When he returned from Washington in 1849, he would have been instantly recognized in any court room in the United States, as being a very tall specimen of that type of long, large-boned men produced in the northern part of the Mississippi valley, and exhibiting its most peculiar characteristics in the mountains of Virginia, Tennessee, Kentucky, and in Illinois. He would have been instantly recognized as a western man, and his stature, figure, dress, manner, voice, and accent indicated that he was from the Northwest. In manner he was cordial, frank, and friendly, and, although not without dignity, he put everyone perfectly at ease. The first impression, a stranger meeting him or hearing him speak would receive, was that of a kind, sincere and genuinely good man, of perfect truthfulness and integrity. He was one of those men whom everybody liked at first sight. If he spoke, before many words were uttered, the hearer would be impressed with his clear, direct good sense, his simple, homely, short Anglo-Saxon words, by his wonderful wit and humor.[20]

The two years in the House of Representatives and in the East considerably broadened Lincoln's political views, his circle of acquaintances, and his perspective on his own future. Nevertheless, in the four years after his return to Illinois he concentrated on his law practice and expressed little interest in politics. In 1854, when the Missouri Compromise was repealed and slavery in the territories became a burning question, Lincoln placed himself squarely in opposition to Illinois Senator Stephen Douglas and other Democratic office seekers.

We can infer that between 1854 and 1860, Lincoln might have altered his speaking and platform manner. He probably researched his materials more carefully and was intent on making an issue of slavery in the territories. Being matched against Douglas, a master politician and seasoned stumper, and the desire to win a Senate seat must have been sources of great motivation for Lincoln.

Nevertheless, Lincoln's overall approach to campaigning remained the same as it had been since his first try for the Illinois legislature. He continued to present himself as "Old Abe," a friendly, down-to-earth lawyer with broad sympathies for the common people from whom he had come. He made his rhetorical strategy clear as early as 1842, when he said:

When the conduct of men is designed to be influenced, *persuasion*, kind,

20. Isaac N. Arnold, *Abraham Lincoln* (Chicago, 1885), 83.

unassuming persuasion, should ever be adopted. It is an old and a true maxim, that a "drop of honey catches more flies than a gallon of gall." So with men. If you would win a man to your cause, *first* convince him that you are his sincere friend. Therein is a drop of honey that catches his heart, which, say what he will, is the great high road to his reason, and which, when once gained, you will find but little trouble in convincing his judgment of the justice of your cause, if indeed that cause really be a just one.[21]

A reporter for the *Central Transcript* of Clinton, Illinois, gave a good view of Lincoln in action: "The old familiar face of A. Lincoln is again amongst us and we cannot help noticing the peculiarly friendly expression with which he greets everybody, and everybody greets him. He comes back to us after electrifying Ohio, with all his blushing honors thick upon him; yet the poorest and plainest amongst our people, fears not to approach, and never fails to receive a hearty welcome from him."[22]

His clothes were certainly consistent with his humble image. Whether by accident, design, or nonchalance, "his attire and physical habits," according to Whitney, "were on a plane with those of an ordinary farmer: his hat was innocent of a nap:—his boots had no acquaintance with blacking:—his clothes had not been introduced to the whisk broom:—his carpet-bag was well worn and dilapidated;—his umbrella was substantial, but of a faded green, well worn, the knob gone, and the name 'A. Lincoln' cut out of white muslin, and sewed in the inside:—and for an outer garment a short circular blue cloak, which he got in Washington in 1849, and kept for ten years."[23]

Contrasting Lincoln with Douglas, the pro-Lincoln New York *Tribune* gives another view of his approach. "Lincoln is colloquial, affable, good-natured, almost jolly. He states the case at issue with so much easy good humor and fairness that his opponents are almost persuaded he is not an opponent at all. . . . At this time, you have scarcely suspected him of any set purpose. He was simply talking about things as they are, in a pleasant after dinner mood."[24]

Another picture comes from youthful Carl Schurz, who followed Lincoln on the campaign trail against Douglas in 1858:

21. Richard Hofstadter, "Abraham Lincoln and the Self-Made Myth," in Hofstadter, *American Political Tradition* (New York, 1948), 93–136; Abraham Lincoln, "Temperance Address," delivered February 22, 1842, in Basler (ed.), *Collected Works*, I, 273.

22. *Central Transcript* (Clinton, Ill.), October 6, 1859, quoted in Miers (ed.) *Lincoln Day by Day*, II, 263.

23. Whitney, *Life on the Circuit*, 55.

24. New York *Tribune*, June 26, 1858, quoted in Mitgang (ed.), *Press Portrait*, 97.

On his head he wore a somewhat battered "stovepipe" hat. His neck emerged, long and sinewy, from a white collar turned down over a thin black necktie. His lank ungainly body was clad in a rusty black dress coat with sleeves that should have been longer; but his arms appeared so long that the sleeves of a "store" coat could hardly be expected to cover them all the way down to the wrists. His black trousers, too, permitted a very full view of his large feet. On his left arm he carried a gray woolen shawl, which evidently served him for an overcoat in chilly weather. His left hand held a cotton umbrella . . . and also a black satchel that bore the marks of long and hard use. . . . I had seen in Washington and in the West, several public men of rough appearance; but none whose looks seemed quite so uncouth, not to say grotesque, as Lincoln's.[25]

After 1858 Lincoln commenced to wear a pair of steel-rimmed glasses. Speaking in Chicago on July 10, 1858, he remarked to his audience: "Gentlemen, reading from speeches is a very tedious business, particularly for an old man that has to put on spectacles, and the more so if the man be so tall that he has to bend over the light."[26]

The scattered accounts of Lincoln's delivery make no mention of his attempting comic poses or striving solely for humorous effects. He continued privately to enjoy storytelling. On the stump he could answer an opponent's barbs in kind, and he knew well how to contend with the banter at a rally. Often he inserted into a passage droll illustrations that brought smiles and laughter. But in his public speaking he concentrated on the issues at hand, sidestepped personal attacks, and indulged in no declamatory or oratorical flourishes, or, in the words of the Chicago *Press and Tribune*, "no rant—no fustion—no bombast." In the 1858 senatorial canvass he refuted the arguments of Douglas, seldom if ever questioning his character or motives. Douglas, in turn, seemingly understood Lincoln's thrusts as sincere and not as personal vilification.[27]

About 1860, Lincoln commenced to pay more attention to his clothing. In fact, when he went to New York to deliver the Cooper Union address in early 1860, he purchased a new suit. The presidential Lincoln usually appeared in a Prince Albert coat, a white shirt, a carefully arranged black string tie, a black satin vest, black pants, and boots. The most striking item of his apparel remained his stovepipe hat. His appearance probably improved because he wore tailored suits

25. Shurz, *Reminiscences*, II, 90.
26. Basler (ed.), *Collected Works*, II, 489.
27. Chicago *Press and Tribune*, June 27, 1857, quoted in Mitgang (ed.), *Press Portrait*, 85.

and had assistance in maintaining his clothes. Nevertheless, his critics continued to ridicule his appearance. The sophisticated English journalist William H. Russell, who found many Americans crude, described Lincoln in 1861 as "dressed in an ill-fitting wrinkled suit of black, which put one in mind of an undertaker's uniform at a funeral; round his neck a rope of black silks was knotted in a large bulb, with flying ends projecting beyond the collar of his coat." The photographs taken during the presidential years emphasize Lincoln's gaunt features and reflect his weariness and sadness, as well as the terrible responsibilities he bore. Consequently, he appeared more subdued and dignified than when he campaigned in Illinois.[28]

During his presidential years Lincoln won recognition for his eloquence, mainly because of five speeches: the Cooper Union address, the farewell address at Springfield, the First and Second Inaugural Addresses, and foremost the Gettysburg Address. The ceremonial nature of these occasions limited Lincoln in his content and manner.

The brief farewell address, delivered at the dramatic moment when he left Springfield to assume his duties in Washington, was extemporaneous, but it was preserved because a reporter wrote it down after Lincoln's departure. Lincoln meticulously and thoughtfully prepared the other four addresses after consultation with confidants, and the speeches were reviewed by advisers.

In delivering each of these addresses, Lincoln spoke from manuscript. Since he had an excellent memory, it is not clear how he used his manuscripts. He read the First and Second Inaugural Addresses, but there is disagreement about what he did at Gettysburg. We know that he probably held a two-page manuscript in his left hand. Some say that after he put on his glasses he read his brief speech. But Nicolay wrote in 1894: "The newspaper records indicate that when Mr. Lincoln began to speak, he held in his hand the manuscript first draft of his address. . . . But it is the distinct recollections of the writer, who sat within a few feet of him, that he did not read from the written pages, though that impression was naturally left upon many of his auditors." Others who reminisced years later are equally emphatic in

28. William Howard Russell, *My Diary North and South*, ed. Fletcher Pratt (New York, 1954), 22.

their claims that Lincoln read the speech. We will never know what Lincoln actually did at Gettysburg.[29]

Abraham Lincoln was not an orator in a class with men such as Daniel Webster, Edward Everett, and Charles Sumner. These foremost representatives of the golden age of American oratory attracted great followings because of their classical allusions, metaphorical language, richly modulated voices, and grand manner. On great occasions they indulged in oratory for its own sake. The dapper Little Giant could travel in such company, but not Honest Abe Lincoln.

Lincoln found his forte in simplicity—cogent argument; plain language; pithy, often amusing illustrations; and an unassuming style. Although cartoonists and journalists caricatured and lampooned him for awkwardness, his opponents knew that Lincoln was a formidable adversary. An acquaintance of some years, Douglas admitted in 1858 that he would have his hands full because Lincoln was "the strong man of his party—full of wit, facts, dates, and the best stump speaker with droll ways and dry jokes in the West." Douglas conceded that Lincoln was "as honest as he [was] shrewd" and that a victory over him would be "hardly won." Douglas could not know how costly such a victory would ultimately be.[30]

On the Illinois hustings, Lincoln made his image a vital element in his campaign strategy. The "poor, lean lank face," the squeaky voice, the ill-fitting clothes, the shawl, and the battered carpetbag conspired to make Lincoln appealing and trustworthy. To the common people, Lincoln became a friend who identified with them and understood their problems. Therein was the "drop of honey" that won men to his cause. Lincoln relied heavily upon the element of persuasion that the ancient rhetoricians called *ethos*: he won support by demonstrating that he was a man of common sense, good moral character, and goodwill.

29. Louis Warren, *Lincoln's Gettysburg Declaration* (Fort Wayne, Ind., 1964), 122–23; John G. Nicolay, "Lincoln's Gettysburg Address," *Century Magazine*, XLVII (February, 1894), 602.
30. John W. Forney, *Anecdotes of Public Men* (2 vols.; New York, 1881), II, 179.

INDEX